VGM Opportunities Series

OPPORTUNITIES IN LAW CAREERS

Gary A. Munneke

Professor of Law, Pace University School of Law

Revised Edition

Foreword by
Robert Michael Greene
Partner
Phillips, Lytle, Hitchcock, Blaine & Huber

 **VGM Career Books**

Library of Congress Cataloging-in-Publication Data

Munneke, Gary A.
    Opportunities in law careers / Gary A. Munneke. — Rev. ed.
        p.   cm. — (VGM opportunities series)
    Includes bibliographical references.
    ISBN 0-658-01046-8 (hardcover)
    ISBN 0-658-01047-6 (paperback)
    1. Law—Vocational guidance—United States. I. Title. II. Series.

KF297.Z9 M84 2001
340'.023'73—dc21

                                                                00-68664

Cover photograph copyright © PhotoDisc

Published by VGM Career Books
A division of The McGraw-Hill Companies.
4255 West Touhy Avenue, Lincolnwood (Chicago), Illinois 60712-1975 U.S.A.
Copyright © 2001 by The McGraw-Hill Companies.
Printed in the United States of America
International Standard Book Number: 0-658-01046-8 (hardcover)
                                                        0-658-01047-6 (paperback)

1   2   3   4   5   6   7   8   9   0   LB/LB   0   9   8   7   6   5   4   3   2   1

CONTENTS

ABOUT THE AUTHOR

Gary A. Munneke is presently Professor of Law at the Pace University School of Law. Previously he served as Assistant Dean at the University of Texas School of Law in Austin, Texas, and as a faculty member at the law school of Widener University. A native of Cedar Rapids, Iowa, Professor Munneke attended the University of Texas at Austin, graduating in 1970 with a B.A. in psychology, and in 1973 with a J.D. from the University of Texas School of Law.

Professor Munneke has been an active member of the American Bar Association, serving on a number of its committees. He is a past chair of the Law Practice Management Section and serves in the ABA House of Delegates. He served on ABA's Coordinating Committee on Legal Education. He also chaired the Standing Committee on Professional Utilization and Career Development and was the articles editor of *Legal Economics* magazine. Professor Munneke served as president of the National Association for Law Placement in 1977–1978.

Professor Munneke has written or edited sixteen books and numerous articles, including *Seize the Future*; Barron's *How to Succeed in Law School; Barron's Guide to Law Schools;* the ABA Career Series titles *Nonlegal Careers for Lawyers in the Private*

Sector and *The Legal Career Guide: From Law Student to Lawyer;* and the VGM Professional Careers series publication, *Careers in Law.*

FOREWORD

I first arrived at law school as an enrolled student on the evening before classes were to begin. I roamed empty halls, scrupulously reading every bulletin board. I was rudely awakened by my list of course offerings, which included "Torts I." I had thought torts had something to do with physics or fancy little French pastries. I had no notion what it meant as a law school course.

Telling this story to other students in the days that followed, I became the target of that brand of brutal humor reserved by college and law students for each other. Thus I earned the nickname that would follow me throughout my law school career.

That incident, although it still brings a smile to my face, points out the total lack of preparation that I had for the practicalities and peculiarities of law school or a legal career. My exposure to the work of lawyers had been restricted to Perry Mason.

Well, law school and my career have been very different from anything I had imagined or had seen (or have since seen) on television. Although surprises may be fun, preparation is better. Hence this book.

After my own awkward beginning, law as a career has been very good to me. The opportunities provided to me over the last two decades are still available to you. A legal education adds a dimension to your life that can be spread across a multitude of interests and careers. Among the doors opened to you are government service, private practice, politics, business, education, public service, or a combination of them—just about any pursuit involving people.

For people are the constant if you pursue and then utilize a legal education. If you like dealing with people and helping people, law can be the great enabler. Law can give you the skills to raise the effectiveness of your help to a higher, more potent level. You can protect the minority community, counsel women on their rights in a domestic dispute, draft new laws to preserve the ozone layer, assure the accused of their constitutional rights, devise corporate structures to facilitate the acquisition of a new business, or teach others about consumer affairs. You can assist political candidates with their positions on key socio-legal issues, fight to protect the rights of the elderly in institutional care, assist parents to pass on their property to their children, raise capital to fund an inventor's brainchild, correct the wrong done by an unsafe product, or find ways to avoid taxes.

However you utilize your training, it can bring feelings of satisfaction, intellectual stimulation, and a reasonable income. Law will probably not make you wealthy, but it will provide a rich professional life. You will face new issues each day, meet new people with new problems. It will not be boring, or at least not for long, because you have the flexibility to change what you are doing and use your training on something that does interest you. That is a wonderful capacity to have, and only law provides it.

I have enjoyed the practice of law. Given my lack of initial orientation or focus, I have been very lucky. I would not recommend the same approach to you. You have already started to prepare by reading this book. Take it to heart; it has a wealth of information that you need to decide if law is for you and, if so, how to go about starting your career.

I wish you luck in your choices, in your academics, in your career. You are taking the correct first step.

Robert Michael Greene
(Alias "Torts")
Buffalo, New York

Robert Michael Greene is a partner in the Buffalo, NY, law firm of Phillips, Lytle, Hitchcock, Blaine & Huber. He has also written several books for lawyers including *Making Partner* and *Management Partner 101*.

PREFACE

This is the fourth edition of *Opportunities in Law Careers.* Since the first edition in 1981, there have been remarkable changes in American society and the world order. The legal profession has not been immune from the events that have reshaped our lives. Lawyers have been involved in many of these developments. Not surprisingly, lawyers have come under increased scrutiny and criticism, because many have been visible instruments of change. The fourth edition attempts to reflect the realities of a new millennium. At the same time, the book recognizes that the basic system of legal education, law school admissions, and entry into the legal profession have remained essentially the same over the past three decades, or longer. Competition is still fierce for law school seats and jobs after graduation. Anyone considering a career in law must begin early to think about his or her options and opportunities. This book is intended to serve as a first step in that direction. Thus, most readers of *Opportunities in Law Careers* will be college-bound high school students and collegians in their first two years.

VGM Career Books publishes *Careers in Law,* also by Professor Gary A. Munneke, for college juniors and seniors as well as postgraduates who are thinking seriously about pursuing a legal career. It represents a second step in the decision-making process.

Although some of the material in these books is similar, much is distinct.

Regardless of where you find yourself along the road to law school, one of these two books will prove beneficial to you. You should also review the bibliography at the end of the book for suggestions for further reading. School counselors, pre-law advisors, and career counselors can provide valuable assistance by discussing your plans with you. In addition, you should consider arranging to meet personally with a lawyer to talk about law as a career. It might even prove feasible to get a job in a law firm prior to law school.

Opportunities in Law Careers is indicative of the many careers there are in law, just one of which is the traditional trial lawyer most people think of when someone mentions "lawyer." This book also recognizes that a career in one of the many fields of law offers numerous rewards, including a chance to contribute to the betterment of our world.

This book starts out with an overview of the legal profession and the role of lawyers. Then it looks at the primary types of work that lawyers pursue: private practice, corporate practice, government practice. The second half of the book reviews the legal education system and offers suggestions on how you can get from where you are now to successful enrollment in law school.

The purpose of this book is not to convince anyone to go to law school. In fact, if as a result of reading this book some readers decide not to pursue a career in law, it will have met its objective to the extent that the reader has gained some useful knowledge that will help him or her make an informed decision at the right time.

Professor Gary A. Munneke
Pace University School of Law
White Plains, New York

ACKNOWLEDGMENTS

I wish to thank Adrienne Diehr, former Placement Director at the University of Texas Law School, whose sage advice in the development of the first edition of this book always led me to a more readable product. Her suggestions during this project were invaluable. I wish to thank the ABA Standing Committee on Professional Utilization and Career Development, and former staff liaison, Frances Utley. They led me into this undertaking and were always ready to give advice when asked. I wish to thank the many colleagues in legal education and the legal profession, because only constant contact with these others can provide an author the depth of experience to create a work like this. I wish to thank the hundreds of pre-law students, law students, and practicing lawyers who have come to me for advice about their careers, because they have provided constant reminders of what opportunities there are in the world for lawyers as well as the pitfalls that await the unaware.

CHAPTER 1

ONE CAREER, MANY PATHS

At a recent meeting of the American Bar Association, lawyers came from every corner of the globe to participate in educational programs, to socialize, and to conduct the business of the association. The ABA, at 400,000 members, is one of the largest professional associations in the world, certainly the biggest group of lawyers anywhere. The 10,000 delegates who attended the meeting represented a cross section of practitioners, judges, academics, and law students. As I attended meetings and talked to people, I was amazed by the diversity and variety of the legal profession.

Arthur was just opening his own law firm after practicing for more than twenty-five years in the largest law firm in his state. He had always dreamed about the independence he would have running his own firm, even if it meant he would not make as much money.

John was a partner in another large firm in a different state. An aggressive trial lawyer, John was a pioneer in the utilization of technology in litigation, including computer graphic animations to illustrate the facts in cases. Recently, John's firm had financed him in a separate business to sell computer animations to other law firms.

Dixie had recently left her job as an environmental partner in a major midwestern law firm to become legal counsel for a social service agency in her hometown. She had done so well practicing law that she decided to give something back to the community.

1

Heather worked as a marketing director for a branch office of a big city law firm in her hometown. Although she was not even ten years out of law school, she decided to function on the management side of law rather than as a practicing lawyer.

Anthony had just moved from New York City to a western city to escape the rat-race of the Big Apple. An English barrister who emigrated to the United States and became an American lawyer, Anthony's practice consisted of advising law firms how to avoid making the professional errors that lead to malpractice or professional discipline.

Bill was a law professor on the West Coast. On the side, he worked as a sports and entertainment agent for a variety of clients, bringing his personal experiences to his law school class on Sports and Entertainment Law.

Lowell had just retired from the practice of law after almost fifty years as a bankruptcy lawyer. He had built his own firm and now was passing on the leadership to a new generation of lawyers.

Ann had moved from law school to a large firm practice to her own mediation service to employment with a big-five accounting firm and then back to self-employment. At the meeting she was discussing yet another professional venture in her varied career.

Mary Kay worked for a national legal publisher as an editor before joining the ABA staff as head of its publishing department. In her capacity with the ABA, she was responsible for the development and production of hundreds of legal books for lawyers and the public.

Shelby started out in a small firm in the South, and later became general counsel for an important complex of hospitals. He had just recently been hired as general counsel for a state bar association.

Richard was experimenting with the delivery of legal services on the Internet. Both an educator and practitioner, Richard was savvy technologically, and he envisioned a day when people would communicate with their lawyers primarily in cyberspace.

Will was a plaintiff's lawyer in the Northwest. His practice consisted of representing people who had been injured as a result of the negligence of others. Although some of his cases involved trials, many were settled out of court after negotiations with the insurance company representing the other party.

Susan had both a Juris Doctor and Master of Business Administration degree, and she had parlayed this expertise into a career in management consulting for law firms. After her recent marriage, her employer supported her work at her new home in a different region of the country through a computer extranet.

Jay was both a J.D. and a Certified Public Accountant. He had combined both degrees in his tax practice, although in recent years he had spent as much time writing, speaking, and contributing to the legal profession as he did practicing law.

Ernie had spent most of his career in the general counsel's office of a company on the West Coast. When his company was acquired by another company and the staff moved to Texas, Ernie decided to stay where his family had invested so many years and build a private practice there.

Craig was a justice on a state Supreme Court, a position he obtained after a distinguished career in practice. What was interesting about Craig is that he was much younger than anyone would think that a judge could be.

Sharon practiced law in the small town where she grew up. After college she had moved away, had a family, and then came back to law school. When she finished law school, she clerked for a local judge and then went to work as an associate in a law firm, before going into partnership in her own practice. Along the way she married the author of this book.

These are but a few of the fascinating individuals I encountered at the ABA meeting, but they reminded me how interesting lawyers can be. They also demonstrated that there are infinite possibilities for those who choose a career in law. This book examines many of the career options open to law school graduates—what they do and how they obtain their positions—as well as other topics such as admission to law school, finding a job after graduation, and the rewards of work as a lawyer. For those who do not go to law school, the book describes careers in the legal field for persons who do not possess a law degree.

A legal education is a rigorous and lengthy course of study. Law school requires a tremendous commitment and is not for the fainthearted. It is not something to be tried out as a possibility by those who are trying to figure out what to do with their lives. For those who are dedicated to pursuing a career in law, however, a legal education is an investment in their future. This book is the first step in the direction of achieving that future.

CHAPTER 2

WHAT GOOD ARE LAWYERS?

It might help the reader to think about some of the things that often are said about lawyers. Some students may not want to be a part of a profession that does some of the things lawyers are called upon to do. Others may be uncomfortable thinking that people may think ill of them simply because they are members of a particular group. Still others may discover that the reality of lawyers' work differs substantially from the expectations they developed about lawyers from public images of the profession. Whatever the reasons might be, not everyone will want to be a lawyer. Not everyone is cut out to be a lawyer. It would not represent a major character flaw for you to conclude, "this isn't me."

By raising some of these issues early in the book, at least some readers will be spared the task of reading to the end. A few may stop right now, and ask for *Opportunities in Engineering* or some other book in this series. Most readers probably will remain undecided. For them, the rest of this book will contain many additional clues that will help in the decision of whether to pursue a career in law. Even for those who are absolutely sure that they want to become a lawyer, the remainder of the book will make clear that there are many kinds of lawyers, and that the opportunities for those who enter the profession are widely varied.

The basic question asked in the title of this chapter is, "What good are lawyers?" There are countless stories in the media about unscrupulous lawyers who found a loophole to get a murderer out of jail, overcharged a poor widow, or humiliated a witness at a trial for the sheer joy of the experience. To read some press accounts, lawyers are at the root of all evil. To listen to some politicians, lawyers are to be blamed for all our problems. From President Clinton testifying before a grand jury in the Paula Jones case to personal injury lawyers soliciting families of airline crash victims, lawyers seem to pop up in all the wrong places.

What is wrong with this picture? If lawyers are so bad, why do thousands of them each year represent indigent clients for free? Why is it that when someone gets in a really big jam, the first person they call is their lawyer? If lawyers are so bad, then why are so many honored for their contributions to society both inside and outside the law? And if our legal system is so unjust, why are developing democracies all over the world turning to us for help in defining their concepts of freedom and justice? Maybe lawyers just need to get a better press agent.

The charges against lawyers seem to fall into four separate groups. The first of these is that lawyers just get in the way; they make it less likely rather than more likely for people to be able to resolve their problems. They actually create disputes that would not otherwise exist. The second allegation is that lawyers are unscrupulous and dishonest. The third claim is that lawyers are greedy; they are so interested in making money that they put their own interests above those of their clients or society. Finally, there remains the suggestion that there is a "glut of lawyers" so huge that like a plague of locusts they destroy the product of society's work.

DO LAWYERS GET IN THE WAY?

Do lawyers generate legal problems or interfere with the resolution of those problems? The answer is that it depends on who you are. Landlords may not want uppity tenants to sue them about conditions in their buildings. A manufacturer may not want to hear that people have been injured by shoddy products he or she has placed in the market. A doctor may not want to deal with patients who claim that they would not have gone through with an expensive operation if they had been advised of the risks involved. There is more than one side to every lawsuit. When one person feels wronged by another person or entity and cannot resolve the problem amicably, it is natural to turn to a lawyer and the legal system.

Critics sometimes forget that lawyers represent people who come to them to help solve problems that they could not work out on their own. People go to lawyers for a variety of reasons. They believe that lawyers can get things done that other people can't. They believe that lawyers will strongly and vocally assert and defend their rights. They recognize that when their freedoms or resources are attacked, an attorney is often the best person to defend them. They believe that lawyers can represent them in a way that effectively articulates what they want. They know that lawyers can negotiate with others to obtain a favorable result. They trust lawyers to advise them on issues involving the law, issues that are pervasive in both business and personal activities today. Lawyers can evaluate legal problems and make recommendations, or they can interpret laws that seem like a jigsaw puzzle to those not trained in law. People appreciate the fact that lawyers will give them unbiased counsel about what to do. People also value the fact that communications between them and their lawyers are treated confidentially.

The basic reasons that people turn to lawyers relate to the special qualities of the lawyer-client relationship. At its heart is the notion of confidentiality. A client can confide personal and intimate details to a lawyer who knows that not even a court can compel him or her to reveal what is said.

Lawyers also are committed to a principle of zealous representation. This means that a lawyer is required to go all out, to give 100 percent on behalf of the client within the bounds of the law. If the interests of other clients or persons, or the lawyer's own interests, interfere with his or her ability to give independent professional judgment to the client, the lawyer is required to decline the representation. In other words, when someone hires a lawyer they ought to be assured that the lawyer works for them and not their opponent.

Lawyers handle people's money; they hold it, manage it, and disperse it at the client's direction. Lawyers are required to keep separate accounts for client funds and to keep records for money held in such accounts.

Lawyers are trained to understand the legal system, legal problems, and legal issues. Clients can legally rely on their lawyers' opinions about the law. Lawyers are specifically trained in the rules and procedures of the courts, and they are granted a monopoly on representing others in court. Although individuals may legally represent themselves in a case, if they want someone else to represent them, that someone must be a lawyer.

Some readers may be thinking, "I've heard stories about lawyers who revealed client secrets, feathered their own nests at the expense of their client, stole their client's money, and royally botched the client's case." The truth is that lawyers are people, and people make mistakes. Some lawyers make big mistakes, and some do bad things. Lawyers who make serious errors or breach their client's trust, however, are in the minority. Though the bad apples sometimes get the most press, most lawyers work diligently for their clients and never take unfair advantage of their position. Lawyers who do wrong can lose their license to practice law through a formal disciplinary system; they can be sued by their client for injuries they cause; and they can be sanctioned by judges for misconduct in the courtroom. Thus, the system has ways to deal with problem lawyers. It may be argued that penalties aren't assessed often enough, or that the complaints about lawyers reflect a broader societal deterioration in ethics and integrity. Those are questions that go beyond the scope of this book.

A final point that should be made on this topic is that people often don't understand the role of the lawyer. Lawyers are required to keep quiet when the average person would be inclined to talk. Lawyers are required to carry out client wishes even if they don't agree with the client's objectives. Lawyers are always acting on behalf of someone else. They didn't create the "litigation explosion"; people with legal problems came to them. Lawyers do not personally set out to delay cases, refuse to settle cases, or employ hardball tactics in court; they represent clients who ask for these things. Can't the lawyer "just say no"? Certainly a lawyer can refuse to take a case if he or she finds the client's objective abhorrent, but as long as the lawyer doesn't violate the law, shouldn't the client have a right to handle his or her case as he or she sees fit?

ARE LAWYERS UNSCRUPULOUS?

Are lawyers unscrupulous? Take any group of a million people and you will uncover a certain percentage of crooks. Despite the rigorous character investigation prior to bar admission, some basically dishonest individuals slip through the cracks and some lawyers fall prey to temptation after they are admitted. In many cases, the root of the problem may be traced to personal financial difficulties or drug/alcohol abuse. If you have an opportunity to become a lawyer, remember to maintain high standards of integrity and to stand with the vast majority of lawyers who conduct their affairs in a way that reflects positively on the profession.

ARE LAWYERS GREEDY?

Are lawyers greedy? This charge goes more to the question of whether lawyers make too much for what they do, rather than whether they got what they have improperly. Lawyers as a group make more money than most people who lack legal training and expertise. When someone hires a lawyer, they hire the accumulated professional knowledge and experience of that person; they purchase, in a sense, standards of performance from the legal profession. They can sue the lawyer if they are not satisfied with the results. Although someone who makes $300 per week may find it difficult to pay a lawyer $300 per hour, the lawyer's advice can make or save the client more than the cost of the legal service.

Sometimes it is said that nonlawyers can do the same work cheaper than lawyers. For instance, in many states title companies compete directly with lawyers for residential real estate business. When someone buys a house, either a lawyer or a title company can legally transfer the title. The difference is that the lawyer represents a specific party in the transaction and is obliged to advise that person about problems he or she might not have considered. The title company faced with a willing buyer and seller really only has an obligation to complete the deal. A lawyer representing the seller, on the other hand, might advise that the deal as proposed is not a good one. Some buyers or sellers may not think they need this added protection, but the additional expense of hiring a lawyer over a title company is directly related to the added value that the lawyer provides for the client.

Lawyers do not make as much money as most people think. There are, of course, some who have received very lucrative fees and some whose reputation allows them to charge extremely high rates for their services. An average lawyer can expect a comfortable income from the practice of law, but probably not as much as most doctors, top-level business executives, professional athletes, or successful computer software developers.

ARE THERE TOO MANY LAWYERS?

What about the glut of lawyers? The United States has more lawyers than any other country in the world, and the number of people admitted to the bar every year is more than 55,000. Still, the question of whether there are too many lawyers depends on one's point of view. Lawyers already in practice may see the influx of new lawyers as competition. In fact, practicing lawyers are among the most vocal critics of this "glut." Clients who are sued and insurance companies that frequently pay the bill often argue that there are too many lawyers. The truth is that poor people in this country remain significantly underrepresented, and most middle-class individuals do not have a regular lawyer to help them anticipate or cope with legal problems. Likewise, many small businesses do not have regular legal counsel. Despite the fact that some large cities have an overabundance of legal talent, just as it is with medicine, many rural areas do not have enough.

It would be misleading, however, to suggest that all graduates can pick their opportunities. Competition is incredibly keen for available openings, especially the higher paying, more prestigious ones. Law school graduates cannot count on their first or second or sometimes even one-hundredth choice. Some will have to choose positions outside the traditional practice of law. Many will have to approach the job market with much greater flexibility than they anticipated. On the plus side, there are exciting opportunities in the traditional fields of practice for those who compete successfully for those positions. Think about it: Someone gets hired for the best jobs; it might as well be you. In addition, a variety of new and interesting law-related jobs have appeared in the marketplace as the demand for legal services becomes increasingly complex.

Even if you choose never to practice law or work in a capacity related to the legal profession, your legal training can give you a set of basic skills that will help you to succeed in a wide variety of different fields.

CHAPTER 3

LAWYERS AND THE LEGAL PROFESSION

A legal education prepares one for an almost unlimited array of career opportunities. Knowledge of the law is useful in most aspects of life and necessary in many. In a complex society, contact with the law becomes increasingly more difficult to avoid. Business and individuals alike are required to turn to lawyers simply to exist.

When you have been trained in the law, the use to which your law degree can be put is limited only by your own imagination and your awareness of the opportunities. Unfortunately, many persons who are considering law careers are woefully unprepared to make the decision to get a legal education because they do not really know what lawyers do. They are unaware of the vast variety of employment possibilities open to them, and they may also lack the self-knowledge to enable them to make a rational career decision. Career choices should be suited to a person's individual abilities, goals, and values. For some, the most desirable choice might be to practice with a large law firm in a large city—for others this might be the worst possible alternative.

This book attempts to ensure that the decision to enter the legal profession will be a carefully thought-out one, and not one hastily made as a result of ignorance of alternatives.

The following chapters illustrate some of the typical career alternatives available to lawyers today. The list is by no means exclusive. Before proceeding to discuss specific opportunities, it may be useful to the reader to take a broad look at the legal profession.

No nation in history has had as many lawyers to solve its legal problems. The American Bar Foundation has conducted periodic surveys of the attorney population in this country. The 1951 *Lawyer Statistical Report* counted a lawyer population of 221,605. The 1995 *Lawyer Statistical Report* placed the number at 857,931. Estimates in 2000 suggest that the number has increased to almost 1,000,000. The age of the members of the profession is younger and their character more diverse than it once was. This change is largely attributable to the fact that there were more than 350,000 law graduates in the preceding decade, including a greatly increased number of women and minorities.

The attorney population has risen at a much faster rate than that of the general population in the United States. The ratio of population to attorneys dropped from 696/1 in 1950, to 572/1 in 1970, to 418/1 in 1980, and to as low as 230/1 at the turn of the century.

Lawyers do not work just for individuals; they work for businesses, private associations, and the government. All these entities use legal services, and so, while a ratio of one lawyer to every 1,000 persons is not unusual in a rural area where most of the legal work is done for individuals, the ratio drops dramatically in urban areas, where business and government agencies require legal service as do ordinary people.

When viewed in the light of the urbanization of society, in terms of both complexity and demographic movement of the population to the cities, the drop in the lawyer/population ratio is not surprising.

In 1951, 86.8 percent of lawyers in the United States were in private practice. The figure had dropped to 76.2 percent by 1960, 72.7 percent by 1970, and 74 percent by 1995. Since 1980 the percentage of lawyers in private practice has remained about the same. Still, since 1950, there has been a 20 percent shift of lawyers into corporate and government service, along with other careers.

Since 1976, the National Association for Law Placement (NALP) has surveyed the graduates of the nation's law schools to get an annual employment report. NALP figures from 1999 suggest that the percentage of lawyers entering private practice (55 percent) will continue to reduce the percentage of *all* lawyers in private practice for the foreseeable future.

Among those lawyers in private practice, 67.9 percent were sole practitioners in 1951. By 1960, the percentage had dropped to 60.8 percent, to 50.3 percent in 1970, and to 47 percent in 1995. At the same time the number of lawyers in law firms of fifty lawyers or more has mushroomed. In 1973, there were only a few firms in the United States with more than fifty lawyers. They accounted for less than 1 percent of the private bar. By 1995, 25 percent of all lawyers in private practice worked in these large firms, and more than 42 percent of 1999 graduates entering private practice were hired by firms with more than fifty lawyers.

Although there are exceptions, most law school graduates do not start their own law firms right out of law school. Even if we assume that many lawyers do embark upon individual practices after several years with a law firm, the number of sole practitioners clearly is dropping.

Although the organization of the law office has changed dramatically, that change pales when compared to the difference in numbers of women who have entered the legal profession. In 1951, there were 5,493 women lawyers (2.5 percent); by 1970, there were 9,956 (almost 3 percent). In the late sixties, more women became interested in legal careers. In 1970, there were 7,031 women enrolled in law school. By 1995 women lawyers were 202,308 strong, or 24 percent of the lawyer population. In 2000, women equaled men numerically in the nation's law schools. This trend is gradually shifting the makeup of the legal profession as a whole.

The enrollment of minority students has increased from 2,933 in 1970 to 24,685 in 1998. This is a substantial increase, but not as dramatic as the increase in the number of women law students. Former American Bar Association President William Paul notes that the nonwhite population of the United States as a whole is increasing at a faster rate then the number of nonwhite law graduates. Paul suggests this demographic increases the need for lawyers of color and for opportunities in law school for students of color.

The size of the profession is undoubtedly going to grow for many years to come. The National Conference of Bar Examiners reports 56,629 admissions to the bar in 1997, up over 4,000 from the year before. Despite the fact that law school enrollment and bar admissions have stabilized since the mid-1980s, the number of new lawyers exceeds the number of lawyers who retire or die; so, the total lawyer population will continue to grow for a number of years.

The face of the profession has changed so rapidly that it would be of little value to draw inferences about the nature of law practice in 2050. However, since the professional career of someone graduating from law school in 2005 may span forty or more years, it is useful to speculate about the profession of the future, even if information about the profession of the past may have limited utility.

A CHANGING PROFESSION

Like society at large, the legal profession is undergoing rapid changes. It seems that the only constant in our world is change itself. The way law will be practiced in the future will be determined by client needs, which in turn will be influenced by broad economic and societal developments.

Are you ready to handle the problems of space law, genetic engineering, and global eco-crises? Can you imagine working for a firm that employs five thousand attorneys? How will litigation tactics change when trials are presented to the judge and/or jury on pre-edited videotape? When "the law" is no longer to be found primarily in books, but in computer memory banks? When technical and scientific issues are handled in special technical courts? When specialist licenses are the norm for practice?

These projections are not lifted from a Star Wars script. Obviously, the profession will continue to evolve. Whether the changes mentioned above actually come to pass will depend on many uncertain factors. What is clear, however, is that these developments will be dramatic in their impact on the profession in the years to come. No matter how you envision your future, your career will undoubtedly involve areas and methods not even imagined fifty years ago.

Who will be your clients? The development of neighborhood clinics, group legal services, E-lawyering services, and insurance plans will bring substantial demands from middle-income clients for a variety of services. Federally funded legal services have provided greater access for individuals in low income groups to legal assistance in civil and, increasingly, criminal cases. Changes will occur in the areas of advertising, specialization, self-regulation of the legal profession, and questions of competency and responsibilities for giving legal advice. The types of organizations where lawyers work will also shift from traditional law firms to multidisciplinary professional service firms that include both lawyer and nonlawyer professionals.

The adversary system is not immune from evolution; new methods of dispute resolution are being tried. Old concepts of how trials should be held are being challenged. Arbitration agreements and no-fault laws lead many to believe that the function of the courts will change dramatically in the coming years. The *Model*

Rules of Professional Conduct encourage the lawyer to act as counselor and negotiator as well as advocate.

Within the legal profession, the growth of very large law firms with many branches, assembly-line procedures, automated systems, and large paralegal staffs to help reserve the lawyer's time for more complicated legal work are already here. The expansion of legal departments of corporations and the employment of more lawyers in government agencies are affecting traditional attorney-client relationships. These organizational changes are touching every important activity of the individual practitioner and the environment in which he or she works.

Why are changes occurring? Many, of course, are brought about by forces within the profession; but in some cases lawyers have waited and are now reacting to external pressures.

Because the profession has changed and will continue to change at such a rapid rate, it is important for students to reflect critically and examine the new directions the profession is taking as well as potential roles within it, if they expect to act as agents of change rather than simply to react to change as it occurs.

In addition to participating in the process of change, both students and practicing attorneys should be aware that their own careers will be affected by societal changes. Shifts in the way law is practiced will mean occupational displacement. Some fields that were once lucrative will no longer be so. Mechanization of services and larger organizations may mean that some traditional legal work will be more routine and less challenging than in the past. On the other hand, new areas of practice are already evolving, and they will provide challenges that are unknown today.

It may not be totally clear what the legal profession or the practice of law will be like in the future. It does not take a crystal ball to realize that law, like everything else, is evolving, not only as to what is practiced, but how and where and by whom it is practiced.

In short, the legal profession will undoubtedly change considerably in the coming years.

These years of change will coincide with the professional lives of people who are just beginning to think about careers in law. While this uncertainty may be frightening, it also represents an array of new opportunities for the next generation of law graduates.

We should ask the question "What business are we in?" as we attempt to grapple with change. If lawyers are in the business of solving problems, then there are clearly opportunities for those who possess the talent, foresight, and determination to address the problems of the future.

CHAPTER 4

PRIVATE PRACTICE

What is a private practitioner? Most people have images of lawyers that have been formed by the mass media as well as by personal experience. To most of us, the term "private practitioner" is in many ways synonymous with the word "lawyer." Today, although many lawyers do not engage in private practice, it is still a fact that the majority of lawyers are private practitioners.

Before proceeding, it might be helpful to define private practice. As used here, the term means an individual or organization engaged in the business of delivering legal services. Lawyers who practice alone are often called "sole practitioners." Groups of lawyers are called "firms." The firm is usually a partnership, and members of the firm are the partners. Some firms may be organized as professional corporations and the members called shareholders. In either case, the members of the firm are the experienced attorneys. In most firms, there are younger or more inexperienced salaried attorneys called "associates."

It is also important to note that lawyers are in the *business* of delivering legal services. Practicing law is a business, and as in any business, the practicing lawyer has a product to sell. That product is legal services. Lawyers have overhead expenses—space, equipment, staff, library, and other expenses that may gobble up 70 percent of the gross receipts each month. Thus, the lawyer's income depends on how much work he or she puts in, how much he or she is willing to charge for her or his time, and how efficiently the law office is managed.

A lawyer is not just a businessperson, however, but is also a professional whose responsibilities go beyond merely making a profit. An attorney is an officer of the courts in the state where that person is licensed, and as such is charged with a duty to uphold the law and to act in such a way as to see that justice is done.

In a society governed by the rule of law, dedicated to the proposition that all people are endowed by their creator with certain inalienable rights, and committed to a system that provides for the adjudication of those rights in an orderly way, lawyers are not only useful, but necessary. The legal services that lawyers sell may be the only way the average citizen can assert or vindicate her or his rights.

The broad general heading of private practice encompasses many possibilities, from the sole practitioner in a small town, to the firm of more than one thousand lawyers. Given this diversity, the advantages and disadvantages of each situation must be looked at individually with the realization that no solution will be a problem-free one.

SMALL FIRMS

Small firm practice is the backbone of the system of legal representation in the United States. Unlike many other areas in the business community, law firms have not grown to the point of employing thousands of individuals. Although there are several hundred law firms in the United States that employ more than fifty lawyers, all of these large law firms together account for less than 10 percent of the practicing bar. While the number of lawyers in these large organizations appears to be increasing, the number of sole practitioners declined from two-thirds of all lawyers in private practice in 1950 to under one-half today, according to research conducted by the American Bar Foundation.

Most firms have fewer than five attorneys, and in all but the largest cities in the United States, a law firm with more than ten attorneys is considered large. Most law firms hire at least as many nonlegal personnel as they do lawyers, and some hire more than that.

There are a number of advantages associated with practicing law in a small firm. One significant factor is personal freedom. Unfettered by bureaucratic rules or the sometimes impersonal environments of large organizations, lawyers in small firms often feel freer to set their own hours, make meaningful choices about their careers, and establish personal relationships with clients sooner in their professional development. In large firms, client contact may be postponed for several years after graduation from law school; small firm lawyers may have client contact the first day.

Another factor is that the prospects for partnership are better and the time frame before consideration shorter in small firms. Large firms usually do not consider associates for partnership until six or more years' association with the firm. Although the decision to join a small firm will probably mean a lower starting salary and possibly less money for the long term, many are willing to accept less money because of other benefits. For instance, the attrition rate is greater in large firms, which often hire two to three times the number of associates than will ever achieve partner status. This can cause intense competition and considerable insecurity among those hired. The insecurity of a small firm practice often comes from inadequate training and supervision, as well as a scarcity of regular clients.

Some of those who choose a small firm practice are interested in doing this in an urban setting, and they face the problem of competing with the abundance of talent and resources available to their counterparts in larger firms. The small firm also may appeal to those who are tired of the problems and inconveniences of urban life and are interested in living in rural areas, in which case large firms are nonexistent.

Whether a small firm in a small town is an attractive option will depend on the attitude of the individual. Some might consider the small town setting to be a positive consideration; others would eliminate this type of practice simply because they prefer to live in a city, either for the variety of activity it offers or for the increased possibility for professional challenge and recognition.

There are quite a few other factors to be considered, not the least of which would be the type of practice being conducted. Many small firms are not able to specialize because the available clients necessitate a more general practice, or because the expense of maintaining resources for specialized research and consultation might prove at times to be too much of a burden. However, some small firms do have very specialized practices, particularly in large cities.

Yet another factor that makes small firm practice alluring is the familiar nature of the professional relationships. Where attorneys work closely together on a daily basis, they frequently develop close personal relationships. Older attorneys are more likely to serve as mentors to young lawyers in a small firm. While such close relationships tend to produce firms where the lawyers are not diverse politically, socially, or otherwise, it is comforting to many new lawyers to have such role models. One result of the closer relationship is that associates often have greater input into major decisions of the firm than they would in a large firm.

SOLE PRACTITIONERS

The smallest of the small firms is the individual or sole practitioner. The sole practitioner is to many people the prototype of their image of what a lawyer is like. The Perry Mason character created by Erle Stanley Gardner (himself a lawyer) and further popularized on television is an obvious example. With no more than his trusty secretary, Della Street; faithful investigator, Paul Drake; and a just cause, Perry sallies out to do battle with his archenemy, Hamilton Burger, the hapless district attorney.

The image, although overglamorized, has some basis in fact. Many have chosen to go it alone because they are fiercely independent and responsible to no one but their clients, who are for the most part individuals. As a rule, businesses hire law firms (and the bigger the business, the bigger the firm hired), whereas individuals hire individual lawyers. Despite their declining numbers, sole practitioners probably will never disappear from the legal scene.

Today, however, it is difficult to be a self-employed lawyer. Part of the reason is the significant cost of starting a new business, and part may be attributed to the fact that many lawyers, particularly recent graduates, lack the skills and experience necessary to practice competently alone.

There are financial reasons for the overall decrease in number of sole practitioners. The high cost of doing business today inflates overhead, and the economies of scale that are possible in larger organizations gives the larger firms a competitive edge. Sole practitioners may discover that client demands may leave them with less freedom of choice about their lifestyles than they would hope. Anyone with a legal problem who walks in the door is a client, but there is always the possibility that one day no clients will come in the door. Many sole practitioners choose at some time to engage in practice with one or more other attorneys if only to share expenses.

Because the *percentage* of sole practitioners has decreased, some observers of the legal profession have pronounced the sole practitioner dead. He may be ill, but he is certainly not dead. The *number* of sole practitioners has actually increased since 1950, and some demographers predict an increase in number of sole practitioners in small town and rural populations for the first time since the turn of the century, which may lead to increased growth of this fiercely independent breed in the coming decades.

LARGE FIRMS

When the law firm reaches a size of about ten lawyers, it begins to undergo a metamorphosis. What had been a loosely knit organization begins to become institutionalized. Partners and associates who formerly would work for clients and develop areas of expertise in a more or less informal way begin to find themselves imposing more structure on the firm, assigning new lawyers to certain areas, and often forming sections or departments. While organization and management of the firm were handled once without much planning or coordination by the lawyers, they now find that they must hire specialists (e.g., an office manager, librarian, recruiting administrator) to give themselves more time to practice law. While hiring was always done in a haphazard and unplanned way, it becomes more regular and time-consuming as the firm grows larger.

The most interesting firm from an organizational point of view is probably the medium-sized or transitional firm. It is always changing, and while both very large and very small firms tend to be fairly predictable in their organizational patterns, medium-sized firms are not. They may try to stay as informal as possible as long as they can, or they may develop formal organizational patterns at a relatively small size. They may grow into large firms, remain stable for years, or completely splinter into several small firms.

Transitional firms, like the large firms, are primarily creatures of the big city. Very few firms of more than ten lawyers can be found outside big cities. However, in mid-sized cities of roughly

100,000 to 1,000,000, the largest firms may be what are described here as medium-sized firms.

The largest firms are those with more than one hundred lawyers. These firms are located in the major cities. They frequently have long-standing prestigious reputations and clients to match. In fact, firms generally grow to such a size to accommodate the needs of large corporate clients: banks, insurance companies, industrials, as well as large private estates and organizations.

PARTNERS AND ASSOCIATES

Large firms tend to maintain a tight hierarchical structure. There is a partnership, which may include any number of the lawyers in the firm, from almost half to only one-fourth. The partnership is most often governed by a *management committee,* although in many patriarchal firms a managing partner retains many powers and prerogatives. In many firms, the law firm administrator who oversees a staff of hundreds assumes many of the responsibilities of the managing partner. Most firms have a committee system to spread out policy decisions and work. These committees may or may not include associates.

The associates are the salaried lawyers in the firm. Although there is some inevitable attrition, many of the associates (and this varies from firm to firm) can expect to be considered for partnership after six to eight years.

Larger firms tend to provide greater opportunities for specialization, the highest initial starting salaries, a sense of security, and a chance to practice law with other attorneys who are generally able to provide the benefit of valuable experience.

The problems of being an associate with a big firm cannot be overlooked either. In recent years these problems have been a source of increasing concern to law school graduates who want freedom both in the hours they work and the kinds of clients they handle. The advantages and disadvantages of small firm/small town vs. large firm/large city could be discussed almost endlessly. There are, of course, choices that represent some compromise between these two ends of the spectrum in the medium-sized firms in both small and large cities and that incorporate some of the good and bad features of both.

The choice is not an easy one, and it is certainly a highly personal one. By reading this book before starting law school, or perhaps college, an individual can begin the process of making decisions about what he or she wants out of a career. Part of the puzzle relates to lifestyle choices; part of it involves professional choices. The type and size of firm, the practice area, the geographic location, and the attitudes of lawyers in the firm will all have a bearing on your life both at work and at home. Thus, it is never too early to begin to think about what you will want out of a law firm employer. It is also possible that you will find the entire prospect of private practice undesirable and will achieve much greater satisfaction in one of the other areas of a legal or closely related practice.

CHAPTER 5

CORPORATIONS

Despite the large number of lawyers who work for corporations, many people could not explain what it is that a corporation lawyer does. Because they tend to maintain a rather low profile, corporation lawyers do not have high visibility in the eyes of the public. Another reason for this ignorance may be that lawyers' roles in corporations are so varied that it is more difficult to formulate a picture of a "typical" corporation lawyer than it would be for a lawyer in private practice.

Practicing law in and for a corporation, as a career, is a choice made by approximately 13.3 percent of the new graduates of approved law schools in 1999. This corresponds to approximately 9 percent of the organized bar who are actually engaged in corporate practice. Changes in corporate practice, however, may overshadow all other changes in the legal profession.

The number of attorneys employed by a single corporation will vary with the size and type of the corporation. Many smaller and some large corporations farm out all their legal problems to private firms. Many others have in-house counsel only for certain matters. Other corporations have a legal staff large enough to handle most legal problems in-house.

An attorney in a small corporation may have responsibilities other than the legal affairs of the business. Some corporations seek young lawyers to handle legal problems and assume management duties, too. In this sense, practice in a corporation provides a diversity of experiences for lawyers.

Whether there is a legal staff, or an individual full-time lawyer employed by the corporation, the chief legal officer in a corporation is usually referred to as the *general counsel.* The general counsel reports to the president or chief operating officer of the corporation.

Some corporations also hire lawyers outside their regular legal departments. Oil companies typically have lawyers in exploration or land departments totally distinct from their legal departments. Some companies hire attorneys in tax departments, in research and development, and in other capacities that require an ability to deal with the law.

The corporate legal department, whether it is one lawyer or several hundred, can best be understood as a "kept" law firm. A private law firm usually has many clients, but a corporate law department has only one—that corporation. For whom, then, does the lawyer in a corporation work? The answer depends in part upon where in the corporation's organizational chart the legal department is located. The answer is that the general counsel works for the corporation as an entity—not for any single individual.

Most corporate law departments have, in addition to a general counsel, associate general counsels corresponding to partners in a law firm in terms of experience, and assistant general counsels corresponding to associates. Lawyers in the legal department may work with executives in different sectors of management, on a regular basis or only sporadically. As in the case of large law firms, corporate law departments of more than a few lawyers tend to be departmentalized.

Interesting ethical questions may arise in corporate practice. How far does the lawyer's privilege of confidentiality in communication with a client extend if the client is so nebulously defined? In cases involving white-collar crime, can a lawyer represent both the corporation and an individual employee in a criminal case without compromising one or the other? If an individual in the corporation acts wrongfully, what are the lawyer's responsibilities to correct the situation?

Comparing life in a corporation to life in a law firm, the corporate lawyer's life comes out favorably in some ways. In terms of salary, the median salary is probably somewhat higher than in law firms. The top salaries are no higher than the top salaries for law firms, but the bottom salaries are not as low. Fringe benefits also tend to be better in the corporation. Because even small businesses often employ more people than the largest law firms, the insurance, retirement, and other fringes will often be more generous in the corporation. Corporations may offer stock options or other financial opportunities that a law firm would not.

Other advantages to a corporate job include hours, options, and mobility. In a law firm the lawyer is the unit of production. The lawyer's income is based on the number of hours worked for clients times the lawyer's hourly rate of billing, less overhead costs. In a company, there is some other product that earns the money; the lawyers are an expense. Thus if the corporation needs 120 hours of legal work, it is as easy to hire three lawyers at 40 hours per week as two lawyers at 60 hours per week. While a lawyer's first few years in a law firm may necessitate working 60 hours or more weekly, the corporate lawyer usually follows typical nine-to-five hours.

In the case of career options, there are many more places to move in a corporate entity, both laterally and vertically, than in a law firm. Many top managers, including a significant number of chief executive officers of major corporations, are lawyers. An individual who wants to move into management in a corporation, particularly a larger one, can usually do so.

A formal consideration in choosing a legal career in a corporation is mobility. For the lawyer willing to move around the country, working in a corporate law department may provide opportunities for seeing new places. This is a benefit that only a few law firms can offer. Of course, the opportunity to travel will depend upon the size and dispersion of the corporation's law department. For instance, a large company may have operations in many locations throughout the United States and abroad. It is increasingly common to have lawyers at each plant or branch location who can handle the myriad questions that arise daily in the course of business.

When we compare large and small corporate law departments, there are some significant contrasts. As in the case of law firms, salaries tend to be better in larger organizations. More important, however, are differences in responsibilities. The large law department may be thought of as a large law firm that is owned by the corporation. Instead of working for a number of different clients, the corporate attorney works for only one. In a large corporation, however, the company operations may be so diverse that the attorney has the feeling that he or she works for a number of clients. Nevertheless, the lawyer in the large corporation is probably a specialist and may have a practice that is much closer to that of an attorney in a large law firm than the lawyer in a small firm. The practice in a small corporate law department may be more like that in a small firm than in a larger corporation.

The small corporate law department may offer some unusual opportunities for a law graduate. The lawyer is likely to be more closely involved in the running of the business, in such things as determining policy and becoming involved in management. In a big company one may have a feeling of being isolated from the action, or not understanding how one's work actually fits into the work of the organization. This can be frustrating to someone who needs to see the results of her or his work firsthand.

The size of the corporate giants may mean that they can offer a variety of experiences to their lawyers. If someone is unhappy in one area, there are likely to be opportunities in another area. If someone wants to travel, the multi-office corporation may provide an opportunity to do so, while the single office corporation would not. In fact, some large multinational corporations provide opportunities to enter the international law field. Because working in a foreign country is perceived by many as glamorous, this is an area that is frequently mentioned as a possible career by persons interested in law school. In many cases, the overseas jobs go to experienced attorneys while the younger lawyers do their "international practice" in law libraries in domestic law offices.

Although one out of ten practicing lawyers works for a corporation, corporate practice has not always been perceived as the most desirable career choice. This perception is not at all fair to the corporations because, as has been shown in this chapter, there are many possibilities in the field, and the challenges and benefits are at least comparable to those in private practice.

Many corporations hire only experienced lawyers for their law departments. Many of these experienced lawyers have worked in large law firms before joining the corporation. These lawyers may have even done work for the corporation that hires them while still in private practice. Hiring experienced attorneys makes sense for many corporations because such corporations are not large enough and well-enough developed to be able to provide training to inexperienced attorneys.

In the past fifty years, the face of the corporate law department has changed dramatically. Although many corporations still farm out a great deal of litigation, more and more of the legal work of corporations is handled in-house. The primary explanation given for this change is cost. A private law firm may charge $300/hour or more for its services, while the same work handled in-house will cost less than $70/hour. In addition, corporations have found that their own lawyers are closer to problems that arise than private law firms they might hire. The maze of federal, state, and local laws and regulations; the need for on-the-spot response to problems; and the advantage of having a lawyer with no other loyalties all contribute to making the in-house lawyer increasingly indispensable to the corpo-ration. Finally, corporate lawyers are increasingly utilized to man-age outside counsel—from selecting, to evaluating, to reviewing bills.

Thus, corporate law departments are growing rapidly. They have turned more and more to the law schools and inexperienced lawyers to meet their employee needs. As this has happened, the number of law students who have elected careers in corporate law practice has increased. Whether the trend toward in-house counsel continues in the years ahead remains to be seen; it is clear that practice in a cor-poration is a viable career path in the legal profession today.

CHAPTER 6

THE GOVERNMENT

The rise of big government in modern America has been paralleled by an increase in the number of government lawyers. Although there have been those who have criticized lawyers for this government growth, an understanding of the role of the lawyer should convince the observer that lawyers have acted primarily as the instruments of their clients in causing or reacting to this growth. The American Bar Foundation lists approximately 10 percent of all lawyers as employed in government service at some level.

Lawyers serve in many positions in government. They work as counsel for administrative and regulatory agencies. This means that they must advise administrative officials in a wide variety of situations including the propriety or legality of their actions. They do research and drafting, conduct quasi-judicial hearings, and go to court if required. Government lawyers in criminal cases prosecute defendants on behalf of the state: and in some cases the defense attorney is a government lawyer, too.

Many lawyers also perform administrative duties either in addition to or instead of working as lawyers in the agency. Lawyers work in every level of government: federal, state, and local, as well as international agencies such as the United Nations. This chapter deals with the major areas in which lawyers are employed. The number of government lawyers is around 9 percent of the bar, excluding judges, law clerks, court administrators, and similar positions. Government lawyers enjoy considerable security under civil service law. Although many either enter government service or are promoted to positions that are considered "political" appointments, they can lose their jobs if the individual or party that appointed them is voted out of office. Salaries for government lawyers, particularly at the high end, tend to be low, compared to private practice. Thus the government relies on a spirit of public service to attract qualified individuals. Because the salaries are lower, lawyers frequently move from private practice to government service for a period of time, and then back to private practice, a phenomenon sometimes called "the revolving door."

THE FEDERAL GOVERNMENT

The opportunities with the federal government are as varied as the departments themselves, and the departments are as varied as the problems facing the country today. For almost every facet of American life a government agency has been designated. Within this framework, the opportunities for employment are virtually endless. The diversity of activities within the broad scope of "government service" necessitates the careful investigation of each individual department, as each is a unique entity with its own particular advantages and disadvantages. A person who would not be at all interested in dealing with consumer protection law and antitrust law with the Federal Trade Commission, or dealing with the problems of rural America via the Department of Agriculture, might find work with the Tax Division or the Justice Department to be the most ideal employment imaginable.

Government service offers opportunity for specialization. Although some would criticize government for its "bigness," in truth each department has a certain degree of autonomy and self-sufficiency. Federal government lawyers tend to work in departments with other lawyers who have the same expertise, whether it be admiralty, tax, transportation, communications, antitrust, banking, patents, labor, or an almost infinite list of other possibilities. Although many legal jobs are in the Washington, D.C., area, the existence of regional offices of many agencies provides federal legal jobs throughout the country. In addition, U.S. attorneys are assigned to every district in which a federal court sits; i.e., every state and territory. U.S. attorneys represent the United States in prosecuting federal crimes. For defendants in federal court who cannot afford counsel, federal public defenders provide legal representation.

STATE GOVERNMENT

For almost every federal agency, there is an analogous state agency charged with similar responsibilities in every state. Although the state agencies are often much smaller than their federal counterparts, the functions are similar. For example, state environmental agencies often track the responsibilities of the federal Environmental Protection Agency.

In every state there is an office of the *attorney general*. The attorney general is responsible for defending the state when it is sued, which, in this day and time, is frequently. The attorney general is also required to advise state officials on the legality of actions they might be considering. In recent years many aggressive attorneys general have attempted to enforce the rights of individual citizens or groups in such areas as consumer protection, environmental safety, and civil rights. Although the attorney general's office, as it is called, acts as the state's law firm and is usually the largest employer of attorneys in state government, most agencies employ attorneys as well, and, in fact, lawyers often hold many of the high administrative positions in those agencies. One area that is often overlooked as a career path for lawyers in government is education. Although teaching and administrative positions are dealt with in another chapter, it may be noteworthy that lawyers often serve as general counsel for schools and colleges as equal employment opportunity (EEO) officers, labor lawyers, or any one of a number of other positions. Inasmuch as a significant number of colleges and universities are public institutions, their employees are, in effect, government workers.

LOCAL GOVERNMENT

Jobs with governmental entities below the state level are often hard to find because there are so many potential places to look. District, county, and city attorneys' offices employ large numbers of lawyers, including many recent graduates. These offices serve primarily as prosecutors for the courts in the political subdivision in which they work, and the lawyers represent the state as prosecutors in criminal cases. They may, however, have civil responsibilities representing city or county governments just as the attorney general represents the state. There are also many opportunities in fields such as land use planning or utilities law, in departments within city government, and in special districts (e.g., water, school, regional planning). Local government agencies, especially in smaller cities, are more likely to recruit from members of the local bar than to solicit applicants from law schools.

THE MILITARY

The armed forces are among the largest employers of lawyers in the country. To serve the legal needs of their personnel, the

Army, Air Force, Navy, and Marine Corps have their Judge Advocate General's Corps or equivalent. The Army JAG Corps claims to be the world's largest law firm. The salary, benefits, and relative security of military life may be attractive to many graduates. Most JAG officers do not serve in the armed forces for their entire professional careers; rather they move into private practice after a military commitment of several years.

JUDICIAL ADMINISTRATION

Approximately 4 percent of all lawyers are involved in the field of judicial administration. When laypersons think of the judiciary, the image perceived is often of an elderly white-haired man in a black robe sitting in a somber courtroom. There are thousands of judges in both federal and state courts. Many of these judges are quite young, only a few years out of law school; and many of them are not men. It is not an unreasonable expectation for someone to move up through the judicial system to increasingly higher courts, although most judges are appointed to the bench after distinguished careers as practicing lawyers or educators. Because of the prestige associated with the position of judge, an appointment or election (in jurisdictions where that is the method of judicial selection) is considered a badge of honor. Judges, through their conduct and performance in the courts, can offer to the populace a sense of justice and confidence in an ordered society that few other individuals can ever hope to provide.

As with government agencies, courts exist at both the federal and state levels. The federal courts include district courts in every state and U.S. territory, courts of appeal, the Supreme Court, and a number of specialized and administrative courts (e.g., tax court). State courts also include trial and appellate courts and other administrative tribunals. Many counties and municipalities maintain courts as well.

Court administrators are employees of the court who run the business of conducting court: setting the docket, notifying litigants of proceedings, directing court personnel, and managing the budget. Although it is not a prerequisite, many court administrators are lawyers who find the combination of business and high-level law satisfying.

An increasing number of law school graduates serve as clerks to federal or state judges. Those who have clerked almost always remember their one to two years of working for the judge with fondness, as a time of growth and learning, and often as an opportunity to develop a close relationship with another person.

A clerkship for an appellate court tends to involve less action and more scholarship than a clerkship for a trial-level court. A major portion of an appellate clerk's time is consumed in research and writing. When a case comes to the appellate court, most of the routine questions already have been ironed out in the district court, and the difficult questions are left for the appellate court to consider. Thus, the appellate clerk is afforded an opportunity to study fewer questions, but in more depth.

The duties of a clerk for a trial judge are somewhat different and quite varied. Most judges are prone to utilize a law clerk as a valuable adjunct to the judicial decision-making process. Law clerks will spend some time in the courtroom actually hearing the evidence and will advise, aid, and assist the court in preparation of memorandum opinions or judgments.

A law clerk provides a valuable sounding board against whom the judge can "bounce" legal theories offered by the litigating parties, legal concepts overlooked by the parties, and the consequences of a decision to be rendered.

The position of a law clerk has the advantage of daily exposure to varied personality types. The law clerk will have the advantage of sitting in on conferences between the judge and the parties in connection with litigation in progress.

In addition, a law clerk has an opportunity to learn from first-hand experience the procedural niceties of civil and criminal trials and to observe these matters "in action." A law clerk's experience becomes extremely valuable from the standpoint of future employment in the legal profession or with the government. Most law firms and government agencies desire experienced law clerks and reward their service.

POLITICS

It should come as no surprise that lawyers are the most common occupational group represented among legislators. Until only a few years ago, they comprised the majority in many state legislatures. In fact, the terms "lawyer" and "lawmaker" are almost synonymous to many people. Unfortunately, this confusion is partly responsible for the low opinion some people have of the legal profession. Yet, there is a grain of truth there, because lawyers have traditionally been highly visible in the legislative branch of government. The drafting of laws quite often requires the mind of a lawyer to articulate the appropriate language. The persuasion needed to pass a law often requires the persuasive skill of a lawyer. And the compromising required to forge a law acceptable to a majority of the legislative body often requires the skill of a lawyer as negotiator.

Besides serving in the legislatures and Congress, lawyers work on staffs as aides, fund-raisers, researchers, speech writers, organizers, committee counsel, and advisors. It is a rare politician—whether a lawyer or not—who is not surrounded by staff lawyers.

PUBLIC ADMINISTRATION

Finally, another area of employment for lawyers in government is public administration. Included in this field are such things as policy analysis, program development, personnel management, and legislative work for an agency (what would be called lobbying in the private sector). Although these positions involve work that may be handled by nonlawyers, legal skills can be invaluable tools to persons employed in much of the public administration area.

Included in the field of public administration are positions with international agencies, such as the United Nations. In a world that has grown increasingly interconnected, service in this arena is both useful and challenging.

CHAPTER 7

LEGAL SERVICES TO THE POOR

Legal services employment will not bring great wealth; in fact, it is even doubtful that it will bring much fame. One who chooses this path may face a heavy caseload and relentless adversity. The primary rewards are personal, and these do not need to be enumerated. Those who enter this type of practice are in short supply. Those who do choose legal services can rest assured that they are genuinely needed.

Legal services programs seek to provide representation to persons and groups who could not otherwise afford it. The category includes legal aid and public defender work, as well as the broad area of law reform. Not all legal services programs are involved in all these areas. Funding comes primarily from governmental and private foundation sources. Because ethnic and racial minorities constitute an inordinate percentage of the poor, minority lawyers who can communicate effectively with these clients are greatly needed.

What does the legal services attorney do? Most laypersons as well as many lawyers would be hard-pressed to tell. The image of an overworked and underpaid gladiator comes readily to mind. They are overworked because even at present levels of support, less than 30 percent of the legal needs of the poor in this country are currently being met. There is literally no end to the work to be done. They are underpaid in that their salaries are among the lowest in the legal profession for lawyers of comparable experience and ability. The reasons for this are threefold. First, it is difficult to justify high salaries for attorneys whose clients have no money. Second, critical choices have to be made by program administrators, and they frequently elect to fund more positions at lower salaries than to pay more money to fewer lawyers. Third, individuals who seek legal services careers are usually motivated by factors other than money.

Funding for many legal services programs comes through the Legal Services Corporation, although some programs are funded by state, local, and private sources as well. Funding is never enough. Depending as they do upon congressional and executive support for money, legal services programs are always subject to the winds of political change.

The turnover in legal services jobs is probably the highest in the profession. Although the level of personal satisfaction may be very high, the frustration level can be higher. Like many other high stress occupations—ambulance drivers, air traffic controllers, school teachers, and emergency room doctors—legal aid attorneys often begin to lose motivation and effectiveness after a few years of continually facing adversity with little hope of respite. Disillusionment can also be a cause for turnover among younger attorneys. Many a recent graduate with high ideals has become discouraged when faced with the reality of dealing with poverty and its seamy effects. This "save the world" syndrome can be shattered very quickly by the sight of a welfare mother with nine starving children who has come for help because her landlord has legally evicted her.

Poor people have more problems than people of means. They are statistically less educated and so they have more difficulty fending for themselves in the world of business and commerce. They are easily taken advantage of. They have fewer clothes. They eat less. They are sick more. Their problems keep them out of good jobs that could free them from their unfortunate status.

Their legal problems grow out of their condition. They are hopelessly outmatched in the legal arena without the help of a competent attorney, but turnover in the ranks of the legal aid attorneys diminishes the effectiveness of the program.

This may sound pessimistic to some and may discourage others from entering this field. It is not meant to be so. It is meant rather to tell people the truth about what to expect. Good people committed to working for the poor are needed. It is important, however, to strip away the gloss that is sometimes put upon legal services work by its fervent advocates. If this picture is not overwhelming, if you still find the idea of public interest practice appealing, then you should pursue a career in this area with vigor.

Legal aid lawyers are just like other lawyers in many ways. They have law offices, secretaries, and paralegals. They interview clients, do research in the library, prepare legal documents, and go to court. They work hard. They strive to negotiate the best possible deal for their clients. Their offices may not be quite as fancy; they may be motivated more by altruistic than profit motives, and they may drive a beater instead of a luxury car, but the skills they must use to be successful are the very same as those required to be successful as a corporate lawyer, a government lawyer, or a private practitioner.

The areas of law most commonly practiced in legal aid are domestic relations, landlord-tenant law, consumer protection law, debtor-creditor law, and civil rights law. Criminal law is not included because criminal practice is usually practiced in the public defenders' office, although much of what has been said about the civil legal aid lawyer could be said about the public defender, too.

Because of the turnover problem mentioned previously, there are opportunities in the legal services field for those who are willing to make the financial sacrifice. In addition, the interest in public service jobs has dropped since the late sixties and early seventies, when a high percentage of law students entered law school because they "wanted to help make the world a better place to live." The availability of positions is uneven. In larger cities where many graduates settle, jobs are harder to find, especially where the local legal aid program maintains some form of clinical or internship program with local law schools. Moreover, the increased availability of experienced lawyers to assume such positions today makes it difficult for inexperienced attorneys to find jobs.

The most attractive jobs in the legal services as well as in the public interest field go to lawyers who have "paid their dues," or developed credentials in the field through actual practice. Aspiring public interest lawyers would be wise to begin even before law school to do community service work even on a volunteer basis, and they might find it necessary to start out in a rural legal aid program instead of one in a major city.

SERVING PEOPLE WITH LOW INCOMES

The theme of this chapter is that there is a need for lawyers who serve people with low incomes. There are many difficulties and frustrations. The situation may be unsatisfactory in many ways, but the rewards are clearly there for those who are willing to make the commitment.

It is eventually a question of ordering priorities in an effort to determine what it is that you want from your profession. The question is, are you willing to sacrifice a lucrative position in private practice for the satisfaction of doing something that must be done? Although legal services practice may not be the right choice for everyone, many aspiring lawyers recognize that they have a role to play in making the vital changes that must take place if justice is to be a reality.

You may have the opportunity, as a lawyer, at least in some way, to bring about change, but dedication to the social services involves some sacrifice in terms of personal comforts. If you believe that you could not be satisfied with anything short of complete involvement in these problems, perhaps social services is the area of law that you would find most rewarding. The degree to which you dedicate yourself to solving these problems could range from an entire career devoted to legal aid, to occasional *pro bono* (Latin: *pro bono publico,* for the public good) work while engaged in private practice.

LAW REFORM

In recent years citizens in the United States have begun to view the law as a vehicle for promoting the public interest instead of as a tool of special interests. Or, one could say that new special interests have evolved to represent groups that have not tended to use the judicial system to protect their rights in the past. No matter which view one takes, the fact remains that more people than ever before are getting involved in the legal process. Some of the areas that have aroused considerable interest are health law, environmental law, land use planning, communications, and government ethics. Whenever a group of concerned citizens attempts to assert or defend its rights, lawyers are likely to be involved.

Funding for public interest representation has come to a certain extent through the government charitable sources, but a large part of the burden has been shouldered by the citizens who are represented. These groups are very often neither very rich nor very poor. Things like PIRGs (public interest research groups), PACS (political action committees), and citizens' committees are usually paid for by those who reap the benefits. These groups may represent diverse points of view on the political spectrum.

Just as in legal services, this branch of public interest law may involve legal advice and representation. Groups may secure someone in a law firm to represent them, they may hire a staff counsel, or they may rely on volunteers to handle their legal work. Lack of government support, tighter foundation budgets, and economic woes on the part of ordinary citizens have made good-paying jobs in the public interest field scarce and competition fierce. But for persons willing to make the commitment, the need is there.

It is exciting to view the significant numbers of good law students who are finding the problems impossible to ignore. This interest in public interest or *pro bono* work has extended beyond the law schools and law students to the organized bar itself. There is an ongoing debate today on the nature and extent of the individual lawyer's responsibility to society to perform *pro bono* work. Is the lawyer's only responsibility to the client? Can the lawyer's own monetary concerns stand before obligations to society? Can the bar or another agency enforce such an obligation? Who is to decide what is in the public interest if not the lawyer? These questions are not easy ones, but they are questions that every lawyer, every law student, and every person planning a career in law should consider.

CHAPTER 8

LAWYERS IN ACADEMIA

Law school teaching tends to be very exclusive and entry into the profession difficult. Although this varies from school to school, many entrants into teaching among recent graduates were law review editors, number one graduates, or U.S. Supreme Court clerks. Those whose resumes do not contain these specific credentials must possess other outstanding qualifications, such as an excellent reputation as a legal writer or practitioner. For those who fall into this second group, there are two basic ways to find a position.

The first is to develop expertise and/or recognition in some field and to be considered a leader in that field. This recognition typically takes ten years or so to gain, but occasionally may take less.

A second approach is to do graduate work at a school that has a program oriented toward teacher training. The better programs have seminars in teaching law, and students have the opportunity to continue to write and develop in their professional areas. Many law schools use advanced degree candidates to teach the legal research courses, either for direct pay or fellowships.

Teaching legal subjects has in recent years gone far beyond just teaching in law schools. Universities, colleges, and community and junior colleges are showing a great increase in law-related courses like business law, individual rights, paralegal training, law enforcement, and others. There are many paralegal training programs, too, where teaching opportunities for lawyers exist. Some individuals find jobs by applying to the college as teachers of these new legal subjects.

Many lawyers assume responsibilities in the areas of educational administration, student personnel administration, financial aid, career services, admissions, and legal advising for school districts, colleges, and universities, as well as law schools. The administrator is called upon almost daily to deal with legal questions. In areas such as equal employment opportunity, educational rights and privacy, and countless others, legal training is invaluable.

Law librarianship is a job that combines the satisfaction of a research and planning career with the excitement inherent in working with the legal profession. Law librarians serve the legal profession in courts, bar associations, law schools, international agencies, law firms, government offices, and businesses. Continuing accumulation of court decisions, rapid expansion of government regulation at all levels, and new legal problems caused by social change have produced a need for specialization in the practice and knowledge of law and management of the materials that are the lawyer's tools. Librarians manage this wealth of information and make it accessible to users in a variety of ways. Technology is having an impact upon libraries in both management and research aspects of library service. Many legal resources are now available in electronic formats, thereby reducing the need for printed materials that are expensive and cumbersome to keep.

Legal research, editing, and publishing is an interesting quasi-academic field. Qualified editors are in short supply and there are many legal publishers and research organizations. Positions may exist with legal book publishers, legal magazines and newspapers, bar associations, periodicals, and other groups that produce written products about the law. Even general circulation papers and magazines may have a legal affairs column or department. The influence of computerized legal research is having an impact on employers in both areas. Because research and editing require a special kind of person, some lawyers will find just what they are looking for in this field.

Even with a law degree, some lawyers believe that further education is important for their career plans. Combining different degrees may qualify a lawyer for jobs in a second area of training and may provide greater opportunity, but it may also lead to the risk of overqualification.

There are also a number of postgraduate fellowships available. Some of these are well-known and others less recognized. The competition for all is stiff, but the benefits can be great. These postgraduate fellowships may be open to persons who are not law school graduates, but they offer unique opportunities for law school graduates as well. Because these positions by their nature are limited in duration, recipients of postgraduate fellowships must consider how to utilize their experiences as they move into other careers. On the other hand, a year or two spent in an academic institution or other agency can add a valuable credential to a law school graduate's resume.

CHAPTER 9

LAWYERS IN OTHER CAREERS

Many law students either do not want to practice law upon graduation or have serious questions as to whether they would really enjoy doing so, although the great majority of law students do seek legally related jobs. A number of lawyers eventually leave the practice of law to enter the business world, often with businesses run by their clients.

This chapter attempts to do two things: to define which jobs are law-related or nonlegal, and to suggest ways of approaching the job market in these areas. Students are urged to consider nonlegal jobs only if, after having made a careful self-analysis, they really want to go that route. Students should not refrain from considering nonlegal employment if they think they might like it just because a majority of their classmates choose law careers.

"Law-related" and "nonlegal" could refer to almost any occupation from garbage collection to corporate management. There are thousands of job titles recognized by the Bureau of Labor Statistics. Therefore, in this context, "nonlegal" jobs mean positions other than law practice where law graduates would have a distinct advantage over other applicants or where knowledge of the law would prove to be a valuable asset on the job. Often pre-legal training combined with a legal education will provide special qualifications in young attorneys. Where it appears that additional training and/or experience would be especially worthwhile or necessary, students should not hesitate to obtain these qualifications. Legal considerations permeate every form of human endeavor in this complex world. The number of careers open to legally trained persons is extensive. Even when not "practicing law" in the sense of giving legal advice to clients, a lawyer working in a field other than law will be dealing with the interface between law and that field. It is arguable that legal skills give the lawyer a much better ability to manage this interface than the nonlawyer. In a broader sense it is probably true that legal skills such as spotting issues, analyzing problems, conducting research, and persuading others can be useful in almost every job.

LAW-RELATED OPTIONS

Lawyers whose activities do not constitute practicing law are often described as working in nontraditional or alternative careers. Such terminology is unfortunate, because it implies that such positions are second rate. It makes more sense to describe the nonlegal and law-related work simply as "options."

It is beyond the scope of this chapter to describe in detail all the career options available to attorneys. Surveys have identified hundreds of nonlegal jobs accepted by law graduates. Those who wonder if law practice will be satisfying for them should ask themselves the question: "Can my skills be better used in a different field?" If so, perhaps something other than one of the traditional areas of law practice would be a better career choice. One should not forego law school just because he or she does not desire to practice law.

Nonlegal positions for lawyers may be found in a variety of organizational settings. Many are in business and industry at all levels of the corporate structure. Many are in government—federal, state, local, and multinational agencies. Some are in quasigovernmental private associations or corporations. Many positions are in institutions including professional organizations and in educational institutions, both public and private. In some instances, the jobs discussed will be found in only one area such as corporate; in others, they will be found in different organizational settings.

Administration and Management

Administration and management of business organizations constitute the first group of jobs. These positions may be found in corporations, in government at all levels, and in private associations. In large corporate concerns, there are often formal in-house training programs. The real trend in business today is for small businesses to hire lawyers who also assume other management responsibilities. Organizations attempting to reduce skyrocketing legal expenses, but not large enough to consider developing an in-house legal department, often seek lawyers with some business experience to fill management positions. These lawyers/managers perform limited "legal advisor" functions as well as a variety of different administrative tasks. Industrial companies, banks, insurance companies, and other businesses will consider legally trained individuals who have a background in or demonstrate a facility for managerial work. Management or public administration positions in government are often filled by lawyers as are management positions and directorships of many private associations. This group includes bar associations and law firms. Some lawyers, in fact, choose to manage their law firms rather than practice law.

Money Management

When one thinks of money management, banks and accounting firms come to mind. Commercial banking and public accounting have attracted many qualified lawyers over the years. Accounting firms frequently recruit alongside law firms at law schools. Given the increasingly multidisciplinary nature of professional services, and the relationship between the law and financial issues, an increasing number of lawyers are going to work for organizations in the financial arena. One type of business that exemplifies this trend is the CPA or accounting firm. In addition, both commercial and investment banks frequently hire lawyers. Brokerage houses have been known to employ lawyers, but this is a less common practice than with banks and accounting firms. Fund-raising positions, which often involve coordinating deferred giving programs, are filled from time to time with lawyers, especially those with experience in estate or trust work. Fund-raising may take place in the corporation, the educational institution, the private foundation, or the political arena.

Planning and Organization

Planners are found everywhere. Extensive training is being made available for the strategic planning aspects of organizations. The field of systems analysis and professional consulting calls for considerable expertise in this substantive professional area, and the legal problems faced by planners attempting to integrate new technology into existing systems make legally trained persons extremely valuable. Although many planning positions are in the public sector, there are opportunities in the private sector as well.

Insurance

Insurance is mentioned as a separate category because it is such a large industry. Positions for lawyers outside the general counsel's office are basically in three areas: sales, plan management, and claims adjustment. Insurance sales can be lucrative work, but it is not for everyone. A number of insurance companies recruit attorneys for positions as sales representatives to handle complex benefit plans and insurance programs for corporations, partnerships, and professionals. Plan management is a term intended to describe everything done by the insurance company in its home office or branch offices to administer its accounts. Claims adjustment positions have in the past provided limited opportunities for lawyers, although claims work can be a stepping-stone to other opportunities in the company.

Administration of Justice

The judicial system from the nonlawyer's perspective is comprised mainly of lawyers and judges. However, there are a great many opportunities for lawyers who do not practice law in the justice system. Judicial administration includes court administration—such positions as permanent court clerks, administrators, and court reporters. It also includes the broader area of criminal justice administration, and there are lawyers involved at almost every level in positions other than as advocates. Fields like prison or parole administration may require other specialized training than provided by law school, but fields such as law enforcement do not. Many police departments use in-house legal advisors who educate officers on legal issues. Some law graduates go into law enforcement as officers or agents (e.g., the FBI). There is also the area of private investigation, for which legal training and experience can be a major asset.

Real Estate

Many lawyers enter real estate after years of practicing law when they realize that their clients are making all the money. Some make the change gradually; others just quit their law practices. Real estate sales and development are two visible fields.

Both represent very risky, highly competitive, but potentially highly lucrative careers. Less visible are the title companies. It is ironic that in many states practicing lawyers have complained that title companies have stolen their business, and now title insurance companies are being taken over by lawyers. Real estate also raises issues concerning environment, zoning, historic preservation, and mineral/petroleum land management, as the consequences of decisions about the use and allocation of limited resources increasingly impact our lives.

Legislation

More legislators have law degrees than any other degree. The same is true of their aides, researchers, and paid campaigners. Many former legislators and lawyers become involved in lobbying for the multitude of organizations trying to influence legislation. Legislative drafting often requires legal skill to capture the meaning of a bill's sponsors and to avoid ambiguity or constitutional defect.

Communications

The skills of lawyering (writing, speaking, persuading) are the same skills required of individuals in the communications field. Some of the areas where lawyers have been successful are writing, publishing, broadcast and print journalism, acting, filmmaking, advertising, and public relations. Although communications careers are attractive to many people, the opportunities are limited and a strong background in the communications field or personal contacts plus some good luck will undoubtedly be necessary for one to "break in." A surprising number of lawyers pursue careers in the entertainment industry, such as David Kelly, the producer of the *Ally McBeal* and *The Practice* television shows.

Education

As mentioned in Chapter 8, there are opportunities for lawyers in education and education-related pursuits. Educational positions are not likely to be high-paying, but the freedom and creativity fostered in the educational setting combine to produce a strong attraction for many lawyers. Teaching positions are available in law schools, universities, community colleges, and secondary schools. Administrators, who may or may not be teachers, are involved in varied responsibilities throughout the academic environment.

One growing field of work is in continuing legal education (CLE). The CLE field has grown dramatically with nearly every law school and bar association, as well as many private organizations, getting into the act, at least in part due to the advent of mandatory CLE in many states.

Many legal librarianships, research positions, and publishing jobs exist outside law schools and the traditional legal profession. These professional research groups and publishers as well as the educational institutions hire annually, although lawyers may not always work for them.

The Entrepreneurs

A discussion of alternatives would not be complete without mentioning the entrepreneurs. There are countless stories of lawyers who have founded businesses of their own and succeeded. Perhaps it is the tradition of hanging out a shingle or the independent nature of many who choose to go to law school. Perhaps it is the recognition of opportunities or contacts made during years of practicing law. Whatever the reasons, there are enough lawyers who strike out in business on their own that the possibility should be mentioned to potential career changers.

MANY ALTERNATIVES

This has been a quick overview of some of the careers pursued by lawyers who do *not* practice law. It should be remembered that all these jobs will not appeal to everyone. Moreover, this list is not intended to be inclusive of all the kinds of work that lawyers perform. The objective has been to suggest options for the student who, for whatever reasons, does not want to practice law. These options are not second-rate occupations; people who work in these areas generally do so because they want to, and not because they have to.

It is also worth noting that court decisions have opened the door to advertising by lawyers and to reductions in anticompetitive forms of practice. Nonlawyers now perform many tasks that were previously handled by attorneys. The result of all this is that the line between what constitutes practicing law and what is not practicing law has become somewhat blurred. In years to come, historians may decide that the advertising issue was the key that opened the profession to its most revolutionary changes.

CHAPTER 10

SUBSTANTIVE AREAS OF PRACTICE

The discussion in previous chapters has centered around the kind of organizations in which law is practiced. Law firms, corporations, agencies, private associations, and educational institutions represent some subcategories. These organizations all represent different clients, and the differences in how they practice often depend upon whom they represent. The large firm is large in part because it represents large corporate clients with legal needs requiring a large number of lawyers.

Another way of looking at careers in law is to examine the substantive areas of practice. An area of practice may be defined in terms of its substance or subject matter. A lawyer may be engaged in a certain substantive area of practice in any of a number of organizational settings. Some substantive areas require specialized training or education. However, an understanding of what kind of law is practiced should be useful to most prelaw students in planning their careers.

Lawyers are increasingly limiting their practice concentrations to narrow specialties, rather than attempting to serve clients through general practice. Not only do specialists offer a higher level of expertise to their clients, lawyers who specialize generally make more money than those who do not. Lawyers, unlike doctors, have not recognized formal practice specialities, although this may be changing.

This chapter covers only a limited number of areas of practice, and the reader should not think that the list is complete. In fact, almost every form of human endeavor has legal ramifications, and so the list could be much longer than it is. Because the world is changing, the areas of practice are always changing, too.

The areas listed here include many of the substantive areas of law being practiced today. There is a short description of each one. For a more in-depth coverage of substantive practice areas, see *Careers in Law,* by Professor Gary A. Munneke (VGM Professional Careers series, 1997).

BUSINESS AND CORPORATE LAW

This general heading refers to legal work that is performed for corporations. Corporations, from their creation to their dissolution, have a great many needs for legal counsel. Although the majority of these corporations in the United States are still small "mom and pop" operations that may use few attorneys, major companies require literally armies of them. On the whole, corporations require more legal work than the general population does. The fact that most corporate headquarters are in major cities results in much lower ratios of population-to-attorneys than in other cities. Some of the major categories of business and corporate work include:

General Business

This is a catch-all for any work that a business may encounter that is not included in any of the specialized areas described below. It may involve such diverse problems as white-collar crime or property acquisition.

Securities

Securities work involves organizing and financing corporations. The lawyer's role in this process may involve preparing all the legal documents required in some very complex transactions, such as IPOs (initial public offerings of stock), or coordinating transactions between the various parties with diverse interests that must reach agreement, such as suits by minority shareholders. Traditionally, securities work consisted largely of corporate formations. In recent years, more and more of the work has involved mergers, acquisitions, takeovers, and other transactions involving the shifting ownership of corporate entities. A lawyer also may work in the area of organizing smaller business entities such as partnerships and professional or closely held corporations that do not involve stock registrations. In some areas, such as health care, law firms have become highly specialized.

Initial public offerings occur when a new company is started or when a privately held company "goes public." The computer revolution, particularly the Internet, spurred the creation of new dot-com companies in the 1990s, as entrepreneurs sought investors for their ideas in a new industry. The U.S. Securities and Exchange Commission imposes strict regulations on the issuance of stock in order to prevent fraud or speculation, such as precipitated the stock market crash of 1929. Because of the complexity of IPO and other securities work, this practice area has become highly specialized.

Mergers and Acquisitions

The practice area known as mergers and acquisitions (M&A) has increased dramatically as the business of buying and selling companies has mushroomed. For every corporate takeover, literally hundreds of lawyers work behind the scenes to close the deal. Corporate restructuring will always occur in an evolving business marketplace, and M&A practice will always have a certain utility.

Taxation

One of the most complex areas of law is tax law. Just like the individual taxpayer, the corporation wants to give as little to the government as legally possible. The word *legally* used here is crucial, because this is what distinguishes tax law from the tax work of an accounting firm.

Many tax lawyers have accounting degrees and some are certified public accountants. A growing area of tax law is that having to do with pensions, benefits, and profit-sharing plans. Tax lawyers are kept busy by the periodic tax reform acts, which change the existing laws in some way. When this happens (for instance, in the pension plan area) every business that is potentially affected will have to have legal help to review its procedures.

Contracts

This large area covers the buying and selling of goods and services and the formation of agreements among parties in the process. Many large corporations devote substantial resources to contract administration. And, of course, sometimes parties breach their contractual obligations, leading to lawsuits.

Labor Relations

Labor law involves the relationship between a company and its employees, individually or as members of a union. Traditionally, labor law included application of the National Labor Relations

Act and other labor legislation. In recent years, other areas such as employment discrimination, sexual harassment, and disability law have grown in importance to the practice.

Antitrust Problems

A final area of corporate practice is the antitrust field. The Sherman Antitrust Act prohibits corporations from taking actions that would result in the reduction or elimination of competition in the free market. Monopolistic practices of large companies are often the subject of suits by smaller ones. These suits pitting corporation against corporation can be complex, lengthy, and expensive. A suit against IBM by several smaller firms was in litigation for more than twenty years. The stakes in these suits may run into hundreds of millions of dollars, as efforts by the U.S. Justice Department to break up Microsoft Corporation illustrate.

Debtor-Creditor and Bankruptcy Law

Bankruptcy practice became much more viable in the business community during periods of recession. Recent changes in the bankruptcy law make it easier and more attractive for struggling companies (as well as individuals) to restructure their debt in a way that allows them to stay afloat and still meet obligations to creditors. This complex field blossomed in the early nineties, and "workout" lawyers, as they are called, thrived on the many business reorganizations. During periods of economical boom, such lawyers do not fare as well.

Government Relations

Many companies allocate large sums of money to government relations, including lobbying and drafting legislation and helping the company to wade through a sea of governmental regulation. In recent years, companies have also utilized political action committees (PACs) and trade associations to influence legislation, to support political candidates, and to mold public opinion.

SERVICES FOR INDIVIDUAL CLIENTS

Traditional legal work outside the business world includes a number of services performed by lawyers for individual clients. Just as a corporate or governmental entity may be a client, an individual with a problem may need legal help, too. In fact, the roots of the legal profession are grounded in the notion that lawyers provide a public service by helping individual clients resolve personal legal problems. And even with the shifting patterns of legal practice, the largest number of lawyers engage in practice representing individual clients. Some of the major areas of this type of practice include the following:

Real Estate

This is the buying and selling, renting and leasing of land, usually including buildings. Although commercial real estate should perhaps be included under business law, by far the larger segment of real estate practice involves land transactions by people who own private property.

Domestic Relations

Domestic relations or family law deals with legal problems of marital or family relationships. Divorce is a common legal action included under family law, although adoption, guardianship, custody, and other familial relationships should not be overlooked.

The domestic relations lawyer must be an effective counselor because of the highly emotional nature of the work. As relationships among family members evolve and families themselves become more complex, the field of domestic relations continues to change to reflect the legal needs of the modern family.

Wills and Estates

The transfer of property after a property holder's death is one of the oldest functions of lawyers. In ancient times, the power to dispose of the family wealth was one of the most important functions of the family head. Through the will, the deceased person could determine the division of his or her property. In twentieth-century America, tax considerations may be as critical to estate planning as disposition of the assets of the estate.

Tort Law

Tort law includes both personal injury law, product liability law, malpractice, and a variety of administrative remedies such as workers compensation. In the personal injury area, most of the work involves litigation, and lawyers tend to be rather rigidly divided according to whom they represent. There are the plaintiffs lawyers, and there are the defense lawyers.

Criminal Law

As long as civilization attempts to punish criminal behavior, there will be criminal lawyers, both prosecutors and defense lawyers. Although criminal law is highly visible to the public as a practice area, it is only a small part of the legal profession.

IMMIGRATION LAW

The last quarter of the twentieth century generated a wave of immigration to the United States, some of it legal, some of it not. Regardless of the circumstances, new residents to the United States place burdens on government agencies, educational institutions, health care providers, and employers. Resident aliens generate all the legal problems that citizens do, as well as a host of others. Many immigrants seek permanent status in the United States and/or citizenship, processes that often involve legal representation.

LITIGATION

Some of the work already described for both business law and services for individual clients may be categorized as *litigation.* Litigation is the work that a lawyer performs in the courtroom. There is both trial work and appellate work. Trial lawyers are often perceived as hard-driving, aggressive individuals who are never at a loss for words. The key to successful litigation is preparation and not necessarily aggressiveness. Many of the finest trial lawyers are mild-mannered individuals. It is a common misperception that all lawyers are litigators. In fact, many lawyers never go to court, referring trial work to specialists in litigation. Likewise, litigators do not spend all their time in court. Much of the work involves research, discovery, trial preparation, and negotiation. A trial is what happens when the parties cannot settle their argument beforehand.

MUNICIPAL LAW

Municipal law, as the name suggests, is the law dealing with municipalities—cities and other local governmental bodies. Municipal law includes such matters as zoning, condemnation, taxation of property, municipal bonds, and the great number of laws governing the conduct of citizens of the city. As advisor to the city government, the municipal lawyer must be a constitutional lawyer. He or she advises on the constitutionality of ordinances and must draft ordinances that can be upheld in court as constitutional. As a representative of the people, the municipal lawyer must prosecute those who violate the law. In some cities this is handled by a special criminal district attorney's office. In other cities some or all of the prosecution is performed by the city attorney.

PUBLIC UTILITIES LAW

In recent years one of the most significant areas of practice is public utilities law. This may include everything from telephone service, to water and sewage, to power. Given the limited energy resources and significant costs, the challenges facing the utilities lawyer are spectacular. In some areas, the public debate over nuclear power, hydroelectric power, and coal overshadows the utility industry.

ENERGY LAW

Energy law involves rights to resources and their sale. In the case of coal, oil, gas, and other minerals, it addresses the rights to the resources in the earth. New developments in energy law have touched upon questions about legal rights to use sun, wind, and water power.

Energy law covers the rights to produce, distribute, and sell energy that has been developed. It also involves the dangers associated with energy production, such as problems with the safety of nuclear power. Energy law involves transportation, taxation, and patents needed in the research and development process. By virtue of its pervasiveness, energy involves governmental regulation.

ENVIRONMENTAL LAW

In a few short years, environmental law has grown from a theoretical backwater of legal practice to mainstream importance— from a few "tree huggers" to a pervasive field that affects virtually every property transaction. Additionally, government regulation has ensured the significance of lawyers trained in environmental law, who are indispensable to many legal transactions. Since the assault on the earth's ecosystem as a result of industrialization is so global, environmental practice today has international applications. This is a practice area certain to continue to grow in the twenty-first century.

INTELLECTUAL PROPERTY LAW

Intellectual property involves rights to products created through intellectual efforts of inventors, artists, writers, musicians, and scientists. All these individuals—and often the companies for which they work—have an interest in protecting the rights to this intellectual property through patents, trademarks, copyrights, and other legal devices.

Patent law is a highly specialized field, which involves protecting the right of inventors to the profits they may be able to gain from their inventions. The patent lawyer almost always possesses, in addition to a law degree, a degree in engineering or a technical scientific field, since understanding the technical side of inventions is as important as understanding the law.

Authors and artists receive copyright protection for their creations and the profits they make from them just as inventors do under patent law. In an age of information resources, copyright law has gained renewed vitality. One of the more significant expansions in both copyright and patent law has involved the application of rules created for print media for electronic communications systems.

COMPUTER AND INTERNET LAW

The advent of computer technology has spawned a variety of new products and processes, including both hardware and software applications. The Internet has opened the door to a whole world of E-commerce. In this emerging field, lawyers work side by side with the developers of new technology to mold the rules of industrial society to cyberspace.

ENTERTAINMENT LAW

One area where copyright law is especially critical is entertainment law. Writers, composers, arrangers, and other artists' work is protected by law. Entertainment law also involves contracts among artists, promoters, and distributors. It includes the business affairs of all sorts of entertainers: movie, theater, and television actors; lecturers; musicians; singers; dancers; painters; and professional athletes.

EDUCATION LAW

Education law is also an area of growing importance. Public school districts, private schools, and colleges and universities are more than ever in the public eye. Rights of students to privacy and rights of access to records have become issues in recent years. The role of schools as institutions responsible for students is currently at issue. Funding is a never-ending problem. Students' rights, teachers' rights, and faculty rights frequently conflict, and as never before the average citizen wants to be involved in the educational process as well.

EMERGING AREAS OF LAW

Changes in society have produced whole new areas of law; public involvement in the law has brought legal questions in many areas to prominence. Health care, consumer rights, malpractice by professionals, truth in lending and advertising, water use rights, care of the elderly, and occupational health and safety are all areas that were unheard of fifty or one hundred years ago.

The emergence of these "new" fields of practice suggests the dynamic nature of law and law practice. It is never static and always changing. The problems of today may be supplanted by others tomorrow. This discussion of substantive areas of law practice barely scratches the surface of possibilities. Lawyers are the problem solvers of our society. Whenever the issues become too complex to handle by self-help or government help, we turn to the law and the courts. If you want to find out what lawyers do, look around. Wherever you see people with legal relationships to define and legal problems to solve, you will inevitably find lawyers.

There are many other types of law not mentioned in this chapter. The list could go on and on. What has been covered here, however, should give you an idea of the variety of substantive areas of practice available in a legal career.

CHAPTER 11

SHOULD YOU GO TO LAW SCHOOL?

Getting into and going to law school are topics about which many books have been written. This book does not dwell on these topics because, as the title *Opportunities in Law Careers* suggests, careers are at the other end of the line. If the reader finds that a law career is not suited to her or him, that person should not go to law school. Law school is not the place to discover oneself.

Law school is a long and tortuous journey. Most people find it is the most demanding educational experience they have ever undertaken. They must read more; they are challenged more; they are wrong more. Competition is intense. Law school is not a place for the fainthearted or the uncommitted.

Law school is for people who want to be lawyers. Since there are so many areas where legal training is a useful or necessary background, a person has not narrowed the field irrevocably by choosing law. Still, some hard choices have to be made before ever coming to law school. Many law students who have come to law school confused about what they want to do with their lives have left it even more so.

For those who are unsure about their career goals, high school and college career counselors can be helpful. Work experience outside of school can also be useful. Many people today are electing to work for several years before applying to law school. This not only gives them time to examine their career plans, but also permits them to save the money that will be needed to pay for a legal education. Furthermore, pre-law students who have worked in the "real" world with its many demands often find the transition to law school less painful than the student who has gone straight through college without a break and is really tired of going to school. (See also *Barron's Guide to Law School,* published annually, with introductory material by Professor Gary A. Munneke.)

THE CAREER CHOICE PROCESS

As a pre-law student, you are involved in the career choice process through which you will make some major decisions about your life. Understanding this process will help you throughout your career to cope with change and to grow.

The career choice process entails methods of self-analysis, evaluation of the environment, and ranking priorities. In other words, a person must know what is looked for before starting to search for it. The goal is to find positions both personally and professionally rewarding. From the time a student first decides to attend law school until he or she finally enrolls, the person is evaluating, either consciously or unconsciously, all of the opportunities. That there are so many opportunities is fortunate, yet it is unfortunate that many people either do not investigate or are not aware of the full range of possibilities.

We prefer to talk about career choice rather than career planning in terms of a specific model because *planning* may infer that there is some magic formula, which will allow a person to map out her or his future with a degree of certainty. For most of us, this is simply not possible. Too much of our fate lies beyond our control. Factors such as economic conditions, luck, and personal handicaps will affect our goals.

Career choice, on the other hand, is a decision-making process that attempts to allow the individual to make the best possible choices at the time when the decision must be made, and to increase the alternatives available in making the decision.

You should approach the career choice process in a rational way and take certain steps in sequence. This is not to say that this is the only way to make career decisions, but it is one way that has worked for many people. If you are not sure about which direction your professional life should take, you really need to organize your thoughts. It is undoubtedly better to go through the trauma of uncertainty while you are in school than to find out too late that you have made a selection that you don't like—where you have not foreseen what was foreseeable.

Self-evaluation. If you are to make the wisest choices for yourself about the direction your life will be taking, it is mandatory that you have enough self-awareness and self-knowledge to be able to make a decision that will be well suited to your personal goals and individual abilities. Only by beginning with a perfectly honest appraisal of yourself can this be a valid evaluation, and this might well be the most difficult step in the career choice process, as well as one of the most intrinsic to its success. Seeing yourself as you really are, and not as you were, or could be, or should be, or will be, is not an easy process. If you don't like the image that you see, by all means take steps to remedy the situation. However, do not rest your later decisions on projected self-images that are not the real you.

In order to evaluate and understand yourself, you should consider a number of variables—among them are your abilities, skills, interests, needs, values, and goals.

Analyzing the market. This analysis no less than self-evaluation requires honesty. Here, however, you are required to look outward, to see things the way they are. Many people are not able to determine the relative importance of the factors involved. However, some that might be important to the person seeking employment would certainly be academic preparation, work experience, and available alternatives. It may be difficult to evaluate what competition will be like for law school seats by the time you graduate from college several years hence, but if you are constantly evaluating alternatives, your choices will be easier when the time comes.

Ranking priorities. This process involves skills generally classified as decision-making. You will be unusual if your self-evaluation and objective analysis do not leave you with numerous questions, ambiguities, and uncertainties. Decision-making is the process whereby you choose or select a course of action among several possibilities. Hopefully, your self-evaluation and objective analysis will have made the definition of the decision somewhat simpler.

When you are ranking priorities, you are creating a list of alternatives, a list that you will use in the application process. Such a list not only prevents you from putting all your eggs in one basket but also eliminates confusion by focusing your career search on certain opportunities. In other words, throughout this evaluation, you are asking yourself whether or not you want to go to law school. At the same time you must consider, if you do want to go to law school and you are not accepted, what should be your alternative plan? Remember, too, that the process does not end when you get into law school.

When you begin to actually apply to schools your diligence in completing the career choice process will pay off. You will need to build skills necessary to maximize your chances of admission. Although some things, like your LSAT score, cannot be changed, any law school admissions director will tell you that in close cases the packaging of the application can make a difference. You must develop and carry out a plan in order to meet the many deadlines and critical dates. Procrastination can ruin your chances of admission if you let it. The main point here is to begin your career planning now.

Few people will be able to go from start to finish without learning more information, developing more skills, or realizing that new skills will be needed in order to reach their goals. This re-evaluation may take the student back to the beginning of the career choice process, or it may require only a re-examination at the present level. However, the re-evaluation process is essential to making a satisfying decision. The most critical re-evaluation is one that deserves to be mentioned.

What happens when the student goes through the complete process with no results? Hopefully, through careful analysis, you can avoid this situation. In the event that you are unsuccessful in getting into law school, it is probably best to go back to the beginning and start anew, looking at other alternatives.

It should be added that this is a process that never ends. If you get to law school you will go through a similar process choosing a job after graduation. The average lawyer will make several job changes in the course of her or his career, and, thus, will have to undertake the career choices/search process each time. If you can develop good skills of career planning early, you will avoid much frustration later on. You can expect, however, to make mistakes in the beginning, to learn from them, and to become more skilled with practice.

LEGAL EDUCATION

Fundamentally, legal education teaches students how to "think like a lawyer." This means that law school imparts a distinct method of analyzing problems. It is almost impossible to escape this transformation in law school. The educational process forces students to sort through complex fact patterns, identify critical issues, and apply rules logically to the facts involved. Once learned, legal analysis provides a unique tool for those dealing with a wide variety of problems.

Another ability that legal education often forces upon students is confrontation. Standing up on one's two feet and arguing or defending a position can be intimidating to many people. Some people avoid confrontation at all costs and end up getting walked over by nearly everyone. Other people respond to disagreement with anger or have difficulty reining in their feelings in adversarial situations. Law school will make you stand up for yourself, or the person you represent, regardless of whether you ultimately have to try cases in the courtroom.

Law school teaches students to cope with pressure or stress. Many experiences in law school are stress-producing. In class, students are expected to be prepared to discuss cases every day, and they may be called on at random. This preparation involves a large volume of reading; in fact, most law students will tell you that they read more just to keep up in class than they have at any other time in their lives. Examinations are stressful; in most classes, the grade is determined by one final exam, often three or four hours in duration, covering the entire course. There is also competition for grades. Since many employers look to law school grades in the hiring process, anxiety produced by this competitive atmosphere can be tremendous. In the final analysis, however, most law students learn to cope with the pressures of law school, and they discover afterwards that there are very few things that life can throw at them that they cannot handle.

Another generally useful skill gained in law school is self-discipline. Law school forces students to organize and prioritize their work, and it requires regular reading and synthesizing of material. At the same time, there is no one telling you what to do.

Self-motivation is critical to success in law school and essential to success in many other facets of life as well.

Law school teaches students how to conduct research on questions presented to them. Legal research does not employ experimental scientific methodology, but rather it involves searching relevant databases for information bearing on the problem at hand. Such research involves case precedents, statutes, administrative regulations, and other sources of the law. It may also involve reconstructing historical events, identifying authorities to support a particular position, and collecting statistical or demographic information. Techniques of legal research can be applied in a wide variety of situations not limited to cases and laws. Again, this is a skill that can come in handy outside of as well as within the practice of law.

Writing is another skill taught in law school that has broad application. When some people think of legal writing, they think of long legal documents, convoluted sentences with countless "wherefore's," "party of the first part's," and "quid pro quo's." Students today are taught to write simply and clearly, to use words correctly, and to present thoughts logically. Legal writing should be easy to read and understand as well as persuasive. It should not come as a surprise that many novelists, screenwriters, and journalists, unknown to their readers, in many cases, possess legal training. Effective writing is a critical skill used every day in business, from interoffice memos, to reports, to press releases. Unfortunately, many high schools and colleges do not emphasize writing techniques as much as they should. Law school, on the other hand, demands student writing on a regular basis. First year students take a course in legal writing. Exams usually follow an essay format. Law reviews are built around the skills of writing and editing. Seminars require preparation of papers, and other courses include the drafting of documents as a component. Law school clinics call upon student lawyers to prepare legal documents for real clients.

Therefore, if you go to law school, you can expect to be called upon to write effectively in a variety of situations and graduate with a skill that you will never lose.

The list of skills that could have value outside of the traditional practice of law could go on: oral communication, negotiation, much of the substantive law, and an understanding of how the legal system works. The point of all this is that school is not a waste just because one decides not to practice law. Law graduates engage in an infinite variety of careers outside the law, but they inevitably turn to skills developed in law school on a regular basis. If you think that law school is right for you, or that you enjoy studying legal questions, do not be afraid to consider a legal education because of the possibility that you might not practice law.

If you are not sure about whether to go to law school, there are many things you can do. Explore the possibilities in advance. If you are lucky enough to have lawyers in the family or as family friends, take some time to talk to them, visit their offices, and observe them in their role as lawyers rather than as relatives or friends. Read as much as you can about lawyers, the law, and the legal system. The bibliography at the end of this book should get you started. If you do not know any lawyers, a school counselor or pre-law advisor should be able to point you in the direction of someone who can help. Frequently lawyers make themselves available to talk to students thinking about careers in law. But bar associations offer programs to expose young people to opportunities in law. Other organizations, such as pre-law clubs, law explorers, and teen courts, give interested students a glimpse of the legal profession. Anyone thinking about a career in law should take some time to observe lawyers and the legal system in action.

As for law school, many law schools allow applicants to visit classes. Many colleges also sponsor career days attended by representatives of various law schools. In larger cities, huge law school fairs are held every year and attended by most law schools in the

United States. If for some reason, you do not have access to such law school representatives, then call or write to the admissions office of any law school, and ask for them to send you literature. Most law schools have a website as well, so Internet browsers can find information.

Certainly law school is not for everyone, and in a sense, you can never know for sure if law is right for you until you actually enroll. On the other hand, a great deal of information is available for anyone who thinks about going to law school. There are plenty of people to ask about the pros and cons. It may be useful for you to think ahead to the time when you would be interested in applying to law school. How many years is that from now? Are you comfortable with the amount of information that you have on the subject? Reading this book is a good start. If you need more information, what can you do between now and the time you have to make a decision?

CHAPTER 12

GETTING INTO LAW SCHOOL

The competition for admission to law school puts a heavy burden on the college pre-law student. There is a certain pressure to perform well academically throughout the college years. There is little room for mistakes, such as a blown semester, a wrong choice of major, or a year or two of too much play. Although law school admissions committees may look behind a paper record and take into consideration bad semesters, each time you stumble you lessen your chances of eventually being admitted to law school. This may sound harsh, and perhaps it is, but the purpose of this book is to present the truth and not a fairy tale.

During the 1990s as birthrates declined, law school admissions also fell. In the first decade of the new millennium, this trend is expected to reverse. Thus, it may become more difficult to gain admission to law school than it was in the recent past.

Law school applicants often ask, "Does it make any difference where I go to college or what my major is?" The answer is not simple. Some schools admit students "by the numbers," usually a combination of undergraduate grade point average (GPA) and the Law School Admission Test (LSAT) scores. Other schools look at a number of factors.

THE LSAT

The LSAT is a standardized test taken by all prospective law students. While it is possible to draw parallels between the LSAT and other standardized tests such as the SAT, GRE, and GMAT, the LSAT is specifically designed to predict law school success by testing such skills as analyzing problems.

The predictive value of the LSAT has been questioned. Some schools claim a high correlation between LSAT score and first year law school grades. There are, however, unresolved questions as to whether the test favors middle-class Anglo test takers over minority ethnic groups. Furthermore, some of those who take the LSAT generally do poorly on standardized tests. Students who believe the LSAT is not an accurate reflection of their aptitude to study law should indicate this on their applications.

There is some dispute about whether preparation for the LSAT can improve candidates' scores. A number of prep courses are offered in different parts of the country. The evidence is inconclusive as to how much these courses will help. Although some preparation can be valuable, it may be that a self-imposed preparation schedule using one of several prep books can be as effective as an expensive course. For the student with self-discipline, this study method may even be superior. General information on the LSAT may be found in *Barron's LSAT Guide* and *Barron's Guide to Law Schools,* or other such publications available in most bookstores.

GRADES AND OTHER FACTORS

In contrast to the LSAT, where one test determines the score, grades represent a complex set of behaviors and performances over a period of years. If a school relies only on grade point average, it would seem to suggest that a student go to the "easiest" school and take the "easiest" major to get the highest GPA. Such a strategy could backfire and leave a person with inadequate training for the rigors of law school, as well as the possibility of an unchallenging and unsatisfying course of study.

Most schools have moved away from strict adherence to a numbers system. In addition to looking at things like extracurricular activities, work experience, career goals, and geographic background, law schools often look at the quality of an undergraduate institution including the extent to which grade inflation has occurred, the difficulty of a student's major field, graduate level study, and other considerations that do not show in an overall GPA.

The aspiring lawyer should view admission to law school as her or his first big case. In a sense the applicant is arguing before a court (the admissions committee) a case (an application to law school). Although some schools permit oral arguments (an interview) most will make their decision on the basis of a brief (the application) filed with the court. The goal of the applicant is to argue persuasively that he or she should be admitted.

PRE-LAW STUDY

There is no such thing as a "pre-law major," even though some universities suggest a specific course of study or special courses for pre-law students. Law schools require graduation from a four-year college or university. Years ago some law schools did not require that students actually graduate from college before entering law school, but today virtually all law schools require a baccalaureate degree. Law students come from every discipline imaginable: political science, business, history, technical science, education, music and the arts, psychology, and liberal arts, to name a few. In fact, a central part of the educational process in law school is to bring together people with diverse backgrounds and differing experiences.

Students should select fields of study they enjoy; research shows that students do better in subjects they like. In addition, since law has applications in almost every human endeavor, one's pre-law background may provide additional qualifications for getting into certain areas of law after graduating. For instance, someone with a degree in accounting may very well be interested in and pursue a career in tax law. Courses that are intellectually challenging will provide good preparation for the intellectual challenge of law school. Courses that broaden a student's horizons provide good preparation for the wide range of problems with which a lawyer must deal. Ideally, a lawyer should know a little about everything, as well as a great deal about the law.

WHICH LAW SCHOOL?

Inevitably applicants ask: "What law school should I attend?" The easiest answer, "The best one you can get into," is perhaps too easy. First of all, no one can agree on the "best" schools. For the record, there are a handful of schools that are generally accepted as most prestigious. This status is earned through decades of high-quality education. If others prepared a list of "national" law schools they might add one or two others suggesting, as former Dean Norman Redlich of New York University Law School quipped, "There are now thirty to forty schools in the top ten." In addition, there are many strong "regional" and "local" law schools. These terms, *national, regional,* and *local* are euphemisms used by officials who do not want to rate schools. The reluctance to rate schools derives partly from the fact that reputations reflect the past and may or may not give a true indication of the quality of a law school today. It is also difficult to know how to judge a school. These following criteria may help you to evaluate prospective schools.

Faculty. Who are they? What have they written? Do they hold chairs or professorships? What do students say about their teaching? What is the ratio of students to faculty? What are their credentials? How much diversity is there? Are they active participants in the law school community?

Library. How many volumes? What special collections? Is the material accessible? Is a computerized system available? How many legally trained staff members are there?

Physical space. Is there enough room to study? Are there sufficient classrooms and seminar rooms? Is there a courtroom? Are there areas for student interaction such as study rooms and lounge areas? Are the surroundings attractive and pleasant enough to endure for three years?

Placement. What services are available through the office? Where do graduates go? A warning: It is often misleading to compare placement patterns of different schools because actual career choices may not reflect potential career choices. Ask if there is a career library, counseling, career information panels, and training in job search skills.

Cost. What are the tuition and fees? What financial aid is available in the form of loans, scholarships, and work-study funds?

It cannot be said too often that a legal education is an expensive proposition. Including tuition, books, room and board, and miscellaneous expenses, the least expensive school will cost several thousand dollars; many private schools cost more than $20,000 per year. The cost factor is important because after graduating from law school loans accrued during school must be paid back. This puts pressure on many graduates to obtain high paying, salaried jobs, thereby narrowing their career options. For example, it would be difficult for someone with loans to pay back to finance a sole practice, which might take a year or more to break even financially.

Some students work for a time before law school in order to save money to defray a portion of their expenses. If you can find a way to pay for law school without having to work or assume loans, do it. If finances are a problem, but you want to be a lawyer, do not let money stand in your way. Financial aid is available through law schools or their affiliated universities. In any event, try to take care of your finances before enrolling, because you will have enough to think about without having to worry where your next meal is coming from.

Approximately one-half of all law students are women, and almost 20 percent are members of ethnic minority groups. Although it is difficult to estimate, there are large numbers of older students in school today who are retired, changing careers, or, in a growing number of instances, homemakers assuming new roles. The American Bar Association has traditionally advocated equal opportunity in access to legal education, and most law schools seek a diverse student body representative of society as a whole. In the next quarter of a century, the percentage of women and minorities in the legal profession will probably continue to increase gradually as a result of increased admission of students from these groups to law school.

The Law School Admission Services, national pre-law advisor associations, and numerous colleges and universities sponsor career days for law school representatives to discuss their schools with potential applicants. College pre-law advisors and many placement officers keep literature on law schools for their students. Even some high school counselors may have some information for those who decide at an early age that law is for them. The important thing to remember is that information is available along with lots of people to interpret it for you, but no one else can make your decisions.

CHAPTER 13

GOING TO LAW SCHOOL

Assuming that you have completed your undergraduate education or whatever else you are doing, the application process, and retained your sanity, when lightning strikes—you are admitted to law school. What then? What do you expect? Will you be able to cut it? Is there something you have forgotten? Do you really want to go through with this? These and many other questions will play upon your mind as you prepare for that first day in law school.

Law school is at its best a mind-expanding experience; at its worst it is an ordeal. Some students find it the most exciting time of their lives, others the most boring. One thing that everyone will tell the law school applicant is, "It's different from anything you've ever done before." And they will be right. But the same thing is true of first grade, high school, and college. Who can forget the first time they went to a school where people changed classes every hour? Law school is different, but just like every other new experience in the educational process, it is survivable.

Another story that is sometimes repeated to pre-law students is that the professor on the first day says, "Look to the right of you. Then look to the left of you. One of these people isn't going to be here in the spring." Actually there was a time when just about anyone who wanted to go to law school could get in and those who lacked the intellectual skills never made it past the first year. Today, this is simply not the case. Most students in most law schools have credentials that indicate that they have the ability to do law school work. Those who do not make it in law school today do not fail because they are not bright enough.

Outside class, extracurricular and employment experiences that provide a broader perspective on life are useful. Perhaps much more than some other professional fields, law demands well-rounded individuals. One possible reason is that lawyers are society's problem solvers, and as such they have to know more than how to draft a complaint or file an answer. *They have to be able to work with people.*

A legal education is much more than learning the law. It is an experience in understanding how to solve problems. Law school is only partly in the books and the classrooms. The heart of it is in the interaction among students and faculty. The law school population comes from diverse backgrounds and, like a good minestrone soup, the more ingredients the better.

The American Bar Association requires law students to complete at least eighty-four semester or equivalent hours. This normally takes three years of full-time or four years of part-time attendance. Full-time students must take at least ten hours per semester and work no more than twenty hours per week. Law schools offer the same basic first year courses: torts (from the French word for wrong), contracts, and property. There is some variation in other courses offered in the first year although criminal law, constitutional law, civil procedure, and introduction to legal systems are among the courses usually offered. Each school has some program for teaching legal research and writing as well as oral advocacy skills during the first year.

The curriculum will vary from school to school after the first year. Some schools may offer almost all electives in the last two years. Others may provide a curriculum almost as programmed as the first year. Some schools have certain courses or programs, which every student must take. Every school must offer training in legal ethics.

CLINICAL EDUCATION

Every school offers some clinical legal education courses designed to provide practical experience to law students by giving them supervised contact with real clients. These programs are frequently conducted under the auspices of local legal aid or public defender offices.

LAWYERING SKILLS

Many schools are now offering courses in such areas as trial advocacy, negotiation, client counseling, and appellate advocacy. These courses supplement the traditional curriculum in favor of practical training in lawyering skills. One of the biggest debates in legal education today is how much theory and how much practice should be included in a legal education. Different law schools may emphasize practical training to a greater or lesser degree, depending on the educational philosophy of the law school.

LAW STUDENT CLERKSHIPS

Working in legally related positions during law school is another means of obtaining practical training in legal skills before graduation. A high percentage of law students will have at least one such job during their stay in law school, and many will have more. Students work during the academic year in part-time positions or clerkships, and during the summers in full-time positions. The work that they do includes many of the things that a practicing lawyer does in his or her job. There is usually considerable research on legal issues in cooperation with one or more attorneys.

EXTRACURRICULAR ACTIVITIES

In addition to outside work, law school offers an array of legally related extracurricular activities. There is a student government called the Student Bar Association; there are social
organizations; there are special interest groups in such areas as
criminal law, international law, and others. Most schools have special organizations for women and ethnic minority law students.
Some schools sponsor student research organizations, school
newspapers, and even yearbooks. Quite often the law school is insulated from the university with which it is affiliated.

Moot Court Programs

The moot court program gives students, many of whom are interested in litigation, a chance to compete against one another on a
variety of problems not unlike debate. Here the problems are legal
ones and vary depending on the competition. In traditional moot
court, each team produces a brief and argues one side of its case
against another team in an elimination tournament. Newer compe-
titions in areas such as client counseling and trial tactics change
this format somewhat. There are school, state, and national moot
court programs, and the experience can be a valuable one for the
future lawyer.

Law Reviews and Law Journals

The law review or law journal is the scholarly arm of the law
school. In most fields, journals are edited by scholars in the field.
In law this editorial work is often done by students. For many
years most law reviews admitted candidates at the end of their first
year on the basis of first-year grades. Today many law reviews also
admit candidates through a voluntary internship as well. The opportunity to gain experience in research and writing and the desire

of many legal employers to hire graduates who have been law review editors are enough inducement to persuade candidates to put in long hours in addition to their course work to gain acceptance on the editorial board.

GRADUATION

Graduation from law school usually comes none too soon. After three years of rigorous schooling in law preceded by sixteen or more years in other educational settings, students are ready to go out and face the real world. Law schools have certain minimum standards for graduation including honors, course requirements, and grades. In the past, grades may have been a problem for many students. Today, with admissions standards as formidable as they are, few people who cannot do the work are admitted. As indicated previously, those who do not make it fail for reasons other than ability. Many, in fact, find out that they just do not like law study and practice.

It is difficult to describe law school to one who has never been there. It is a complex and challenging experience, but one that inevitably changes those who go through it by transforming their habits and the ways they think. There are several good books on the law school experience mentioned in the bibliography, including *Barron's How to Succeed in Law School,* by this author. Reading these or visiting law school classes will help you to understand more of what to expect. The only way, however, that you will really know what law school is like is to go there yourself.

CHAPTER 14

AFTER GRADUATION FROM LAW SCHOOL

The end of law school is not the end of the process of becoming a lawyer. Graduates must pass the bar examination before they are licensed and find a job. Most lawyers opt to take continuing legal education courses and to grow professionally throughout their careers.

THE BAR EXAM

The first hurdle after graduation is the bar exam. Although there are careers that do not require a law license, it is necessary to pass the bar in order to practice law. Some graduates who do not even plan to practice law take the bar exam just to get it behind them.

The requirements and examinations vary from state to state, as do pass rates. Most states include a common section, the Multistate Bar Exam, a multiple choice test, which is combined with essay questions based on state law.

Strict procedures, tiresome forms, and character and fitness investigations can make the bar application process a tedious ordeal. Although attempts to prevent individuals from taking bar exams on the basis of lifestyle or political persuasion have been unsuccessful, persons who have been convicted of serious crimes or engaged in morally repugnant activities may have difficulty being certified to take the exam.

Bar review courses are available to bar examinees in most states. These courses are designed to acquaint those taking the bar with what to expect. They are not required, but most graduates who have invested three or four years in law school tend to play the percentages and take the course.

Bar examinations have been criticized in recent years. The suggestion has been made that use of the bar exam is supported by practicing lawyers to reduce competition and discourage mobility. From time to time, proposals for the creation of a national bar exam arise, but the Multistate is as close as anyone has come to succeeding. Like the LSAT, bar exams also have been criticized for discriminating against minority groups. Almost all states require persons taking the bar to have graduated from a law school approved by the American Bar Association. Periodically, graduates of unapproved law schools apply to take the bar on the grounds that this requirement is unfair. These applications have for the most part been unsuccessful. This fact alone should deter most pre-law students from enrolling in non-ABA approved law schools. In addition, a school's quality of education is generally considered by legal educators to be open to question until or unless the school gains ABA approval.

PREDICTIONS OF EMPLOYMENT PROSPECTS

It is difficult to predict what the job market will be like in the future—three, five, or even ten years down the road. Any projection of the market would be more subject to change than a weather forecast. Since so many pre-law students want to know what their prospects will be, it may be worthwhile to offer a few observations.

Every year there appear more than a few articles describing the employment prospects for new lawyers as dismal at best. The titles are always a somber "New Lawyers Flood the Market," or something equally frightening. The articles seem to suggest that law students who didn't graduate in the top 10 percent at one of the top ten schools had better plan to make their livelihoods in some other field.

These articles are often simplistic in their analysis and may miss both the nature and extent of the problem. They strike terror into the hearts of law students and pre-law students as well. There is no way to determine how many good prospects have been deterred from even applying to law school because of such stories.

The "placement scare" stories almost always juxtapose employment predictions by the U.S. Department of Labor, Bureau of Labor Statistics, and the actual number of law graduates, suggesting an acute overabundance of new lawyers. BLS projections vary widely from year to year, and have not tended to represent the job market for new law graduates. The BLS attempts to predict growth in the profession on the basis of 1) national economic trends, 2) reports of various state and federal employment and research agencies, and 3) replacement for those who leave the profession due to death or retirement, or to enter another profession.

The Bureau of Labor Statistics states that its "projections tend to be conservatively biased." Thus, for growing professions the outlook may be better than projected. A more serious problem for BLS is how it defines "the legal profession."

If the term "legal profession" is used in its narrowest sense, many jobs that are filled by lawyers may not be included, and projections based on a narrow definition will appear less optimistic. Many of the 20 percent who graduated from part-time programs returned to jobs they held prior to law school, and thus did not enter the job market. There are many things that lawyers can and do choose to do outside of the practice of law. In fact, as society becomes more complex, there are increasingly fewer endeavors for which knowledge of law or a law degree do not provide tangible benefits.

In addition, some law school graduates do not take or pass a bar exam and cannot compete for legal jobs; other graduates simply do not enter the job market at all. Thus, projections of legal employment frequently do not tell the whole story.

If law school graduates are unemployed or underemployed, it is not because there are not opportunities. It is not because there are no societal needs for more legal services for presently underrepresented groups. The problem is, rather, one of distribution. There are too many applicants in some areas already saturated with attorneys, and too few in other areas where there are unmet demands.

The National Association for Law Placement (NALP) Employment Survey gives a clear picture of the demand for legal services as reflected in the jobs accepted by the nation's law graduates. The 1999 NALP Employment Survey covering 173 law schools, reports the employment status of 35,456 graduates. Of these, 32,016 of those qualified and seeking employment, are, in fact, employed in law-related positions six to eight months after graduation.

These percentages and the percentages for the various types of jobs have remained relatively stable over the twenty years NALP has conducted this survey. Different schools may differ considerably as to the employment picture for their graduates depending upon the employers they serve. For example, schools in Washington, DC, may have a higher percentage of students go to work for the federal government. Other schools may have employment patterns that vary with the geographic area or the educational program of the school.

Questions have been raised about the employment situation for women and minorities, since the number of graduates of each group has increased in recent years. There may be substantial differences in employment choices; minorities, for instance, may be more likely to enter public service or government service and less likely to enter private practice than nonminorities. Women may be more likely to accept judicial clerkships and less likely to be self-employed than men.

Geographically, more respondents to the NALP survey settled in the Northeast, although this may simply demonstrate that that is the region with the largest law student population, since most law students go to work in the geographic area where their school is located. The NALP survey shows that the vast majority of law graduates settle in urban areas. The ten leading cities where respondents to the NALP survey settled were: 1) New York City, 2) Washington, DC, 3) Chicago, 4) Los Angeles, 5) Boston, 6) Houston, 7) San Francisco, 8) Atlanta, 9) Philadelphia, 10) Dallas-Ft. Worth.

Many law students who have difficulty finding a job have placed strict geographic limitations on their job search, are unnecessarily restrictive or unrealistic as to the jobs they will consider, or begin the process so late in their law school careers that many options are foreclosed by the time they begin to search. Despite some predictions to the contrary, law school graduates who plan carefully, pursue the job search diligently, and maintain a degree of flexibility can find legally related work.

What about the 1,715 graduates (4.8 percent) from the class of 1999 who were listed as unemployed, according to the NALP Survey? Is this figure one that should cause concern among pre-law students? The answer is that out of any group of individuals, some will have difficulty finding a job. This number is actually quite small, given the unemployment level of the U.S. population at large.

It should be obvious that the job search is tough. It's hard work and it's not always good for the ego. There *is* limited access to the positions that are most prestigious and remunerative. In 1999, 19.5

percent of the graduates went to work in law firms that employed more than one hundred lawyers. Only 11.2 percent accepted prestigious judicial clerkships. In fact, the 55.1 percent in private practice is just more than half the class.

Each individual must assess her or his marketability in light of the demand for someone with the skills and background possessed, as well as assess overall trends in the employment picture. Some students will inevitably have to look longer and harder for a job than others.

Many factors influence these trends and affect to some degree the demand for legal services. Several factors will tend to increase demand:

- Plans to bring legal services to middle-income groups.
- The continued existence of government regulation at all levels.
- The increase in the public's willingness to litigate as awareness of individual and collective rights becomes much more widely understood.
- The increase in the population itself, including the immigration into this country of large numbers of non-English speaking individuals.
- The expansion of the business community as further industrialization of our society occurs.
- The development of new areas of law practice such as computer and Internet law.
- Expansion of existing public service opportunities such as legal services to underprivileged persons, teaching, and administrative work in areas outside law schools and judicially mandated criminal defense work.

Although some of these areas are not growing as rapidly as some predicted and many hoped, there has been and will continue to be an increase in the demand for services and more than enough interested students to fill new jobs.

On the other hand, several factors are working to contract the opportunities in the legal profession. The development of paraprofessionals and the increased use of technology and management procedures cut into the work previously done by associates. With rising salaries for law graduates, many employers seriously consider alternatives to the employment of recent law graduates. Additionally, lawyers must compete with increasing regularity with service providers from other professions. Not the least of these alternative service providers are organizations that sell law-related services and information online.

Another development cutting into the legal job market may be termed the crisis in confidence. The public's opinion of lawyers has reached an all-time low. Banks, title companies, savings and loan associations, and accounting firms are all promising to do work presently or in the recent past done by lawyers both cheaper and better. Less work means fewer jobs, and this trend raises important issues as to what the role of the lawyer should be. The ability of the legal profession to deliver its services is extremely important to the continued growth of the profession.

There are also shifts in demand, some of rather short duration, some of long range. Population movement is always taking place, and lawyers will follow the people. Many factors such as the relative wealth of the population, or the existence of business and government entities in the community, provide barometers of demand for legal service and provide clues as to the need for more attorneys.

The business cycle can affect demand; the economy has its ups and downs, and since legal work is often tied to business activity, the legal profession rises and falls with the economy, not only nationally but locally as well.

Shifts in the demand for legal services may occur in some substantive areas of law. A major new piece of legislation to pass Congress may result in many new jobs for lawyers. A recession could wipe out lawyers who have real estate practices, while the bankruptcy lawyers stay busy.

Tomorrow? Who knows? If law school administrators knew what areas would be in demand in ten years they would plan the curriculum accordingly. A few predictions may help:

- Many rural areas of our country will experience a severe shortage of attorneys as the urbanization of America continues to expand.
- Significantly more lawyers will be hired by business and industry to positions traditionally held by nonlawyers. Some of these positions will eventually require a law degree as a prerequisite to being hired.
- The face of private practice will undergo unprecedented changes with the establishment of large legal clinics and multioffice corporate megafirms, resulting in more jobs.
- The Sunbelt growth will mean a much slower rate of growth and in many cases a decline in employment opportunities in the Northeast and Midwest. For the next quarter of a century, we will witness the blossoming of cities from Jacksonville to San Diego, and an increasingly larger percentage of jobs will be found in Sunbelt cities.
- Technology and the management of information will have a major impact on the way legal services are provided, on the quality of those services, and on the opportunities for practicing lawyers as well as prospective lawyers.

This discussion of the job market implies that there is not a single job market in the legal profession, but many. There are job markets for different types of law and different kinds of employers. There are frequently different job markets in different regions and cities. The fact that there is no national bar exam tends to accentuate the regional hiring patterns of employers. On the other hand, many areas of the practice of law do not vary substantially from region to region.

What this means is that geographic choices of where to live after graduation, and perhaps where to attend law school, can be important. If there is any area of practice you are interested in, you may have to make geographical choices with that in mind. Many people are not as concerned with what they practice as where they live. Some law graduates accept jobs they would not otherwise choose, because they want to live in a certain city. There are a number of cities that are very popular places to live, thus they are inundated with lawyers. An individual with some geographic flexibility will find the task of securing employment much easier than one who doggedly tries to stay in an overcrowded market.

FINANCIAL REWARDS

One of the reasons people choose to go to law school is for the financial rewards. An old lawyer once told the author, who was in law school at the time, "Son, if you want to get rich, get out of this business. Lawyers may work for rich people, but you don't get rich practicing law." There are wealthy lawyers, but many of them have gained their fortunes through business enterprises outside the practice of law. Outside of a handful of lawyers with unusual practices, most lawyers can expect to have a comfortable living, but not fantastic riches.

Beginning Salaries

It will probably come as no surprise that starting salaries have risen along with the cost of everything else. It takes more money to live these days, and recent law graduates feel this as acutely as anyone, especially if they have educational loans to repay.

For potential employers, the question of how much to pay is difficult. Placement directors frequently hear phrases like "the going rate," "competitive," or "comparable to similar firms in our location." The truth is that starting salaries vary considerably. For example, NALP reported that for 1999 that starting salaries ranged from less than $20,000 to more than $100,000. The median starting salary in 1999 was $50,000. The highest average starting salaries were paid by very large firms in New York City and other metropolitan areas.

Because of the wide range in legal salaries, it may be difficult for an individual to know what to expect. There are a number of factors to consider. The scale is generally highest in the big cities; in fact, the larger the city, the higher salaries tend to be. Higher salaries are typically given to new lawyers by larger organizations, although small organizations may be required to pay competitively if they expect to compete with larger employers. The competition for students at the top of their classes may have attenuated the salary range over the years.

Mature Incomes

Salaries for experienced attorneys are even more difficult to pinpoint than starting salaries. There are lawyers who have practiced twenty years who barely earn enough to stay alive; there are others whose incomes run into seven figures. The typical lawyer may earn between $100,000 and $150,000, although the top incomes are considerably higher. Approximately half of the lawyers in the United States have been licensed for ten years or fewer, and these lawyers, who earn the least income, are included in the figures. Surveys of law firms partners indicate that most earn from one hundred thousand to several hundred thousand dollars, and some even more.

Student Incomes

Salaries for law students who are still in school can be determined to some extent by comparison with other employers, but also by using an easy formula based on an associate's probable starting salary. Generally, summer and part-time law clerks can expect to make two-thirds to three-fourths what an employer would pay a newly licensed attorney to go to work. The actual ranges of these salaries is more like one-half to nine-tenths, but the two-thirds to three-fourths figure is a good rule of thumb, using two-thirds for first-year students, and three-fourths for second-year students. Law clerk salaries may be described in terms of hourly, weekly, or monthly rates, and may range from a fairly good income to as low as minimum wage.

Employers must continue to grow to meet the needs of their clients, and many will be willing to compete fiercely to attract the best possible legal talent. Inflation will continue to affect salaries as well, so employers can expect average starting salaries to continue to rise. On the other hand, the large number of law school graduates today undoubtedly depress the salary scale to some degree.

How Important Is Money?

Another way of looking at the financial picture is to compare two individuals, one who worked in a factory from the time he or she graduated from high school, and the other who went to college and law school, and then went to work in the highest-paying law firm around. If the plant worker earned one-half of what the lawyer earned, the plant worker would have made more than $100,000 before the lawyer ever passed the bar. It would not be until the fifteenth year after high school that the lawyer's income would pass the plant worker's. In time, the lawyer might come out ahead financially, but some students may not want to delay gratification that long. Furthermore, since most new law graduates do not command the top salaries, it would take some lawyers much longer to catch up, and others never would. In summary, money alone is not a reason to choose a legal career. While monetary rewards will be adequate, those who expect highly lucrative opportunities may well be disappointed.

JOB SATISFACTION

There is a myth in the legal profession that lawyers keep one job throughout their legal careers. If this was ever true, it certainly is not today. The average lawyer will hold five to eight jobs in the forty years between law school graduation and retirement, and a high percentage of attorneys will make at least one major career change in their lives.

Evidence of rampant job dissatisfaction in America is easy to find. Studs Terkel, a lawyer himself, suggested in his book *Working* that job dissatisfaction is pervasive in our society. He found that, though people seemed happy in their work, they were not necessarily so happy in their present *positions;* they were often on the road to somewhere and passing time in their present circumstances. It is clear that lawyers are not alone in this state of mind. However, it would be unwise to assume that dissatisfaction in the legal profession is completely due to our changing times, or sunspot activity, or some other global cause.

In many ways the legal profession is unique. The dissatisfaction of lawyers with their professional lives can be explained, if not totally understood. However, dissatisfaction is the stuff that progress is made of, that careers grow on, that futures are built with. Find a man or woman who is completely happy in a job and you will find someone who has no dreams. Each of us is in one sense always in the job market. There are very few who would not leave what they are doing if some golden opportunity were to develop.

One of America's foremost career theorists, John L. Holland, explained that high levels of job dissatisfaction, or dissonance, as he called it, will produce one of three responses: to change ourselves, to change our environment, or to leave the environment. When we change ourselves, we accept whatever it was that was bothering us. When we change the environment, we eliminate the offending problem. If neither adjustment is possible, we look for something new. For instance, if a lawyer is told he or she will not be made a partner in the law firm but can stay as an associate, the lawyer will either accept the decision, attempt to prove that he or she should be made partner, or pull out an old resume and start to revise it.

Career decisions are almost always complex ones involving many considerations. Factors such as the employability of the individual in the marketplace, tolerance for the bad situation, willingness to assume a risk, and the need for security inevitably weigh heavily in the equation. Each year thousands of lawyers change jobs. In many instances, the transition is smooth, but very often the change is difficult and painful. Sometimes it is destructive.

What are the roots of lawyer dissatisfaction? The most commonly named reason given by dissatisfied lawyers is that their present employment did not utilize the skills they believed they possessed as lawyers. It is important to note that most of these people held legal jobs that would appear to be attractive on paper. A second cause of dissatisfaction is low salary and/or a perception that the position had "no future." A third complaint is unpleasant working conditions, including conflicts with supervising attorneys.

The term "underemployed" has been applied to lawyers who 1) practice law and do not have enough legal work to stay busy full-time, or 2) are employed in nonlegal positions, having been unable to obtain a legal one.

The term "underemployment" is too subjective to be useful in discussing the broad range of job dissatisfaction. How many lawyers would call themselves underemployed whose jobs would be considered ideal by others? How many who would call themselves underemployed could charitably be described as overemployed by an unbiased outsider? How many in jobs with "low status" are perfectly happy? How many could have a better job if they would be willing to move to another city? How many of those without legal work do not operate an efficient law office, or never learned to attract and keep clients?

It is better to focus attention on specific job-related factors that have a major bearing on whether one will be happy in his or her job or seek a new one. Focusing on the three reasons articulated above, it is possible to get a clearer picture of situations where a lawyer would be willing to make a job change whether that person is in a legal or nonlegal job.

The first complaint, of not using the skills one possesses or learns in law school, is most critical. Holland, in *Making Vocational Choices,* articulates the theory that individuals tend to like what they succeed at, and that they will succeed in the future in activities utilizing the same skills and activities they have succeeded at in the past. In other words, career development ought to involve careful evaluation of past personal and job behavior to determine competencies that will be most likely to produce success in a new situation.

Lack of job future and salary are often related and have been grouped together for purposes of this discussion. Having a feeling that a job contributes to a positive direction in one's career is essential to one's self-concept and job satisfaction. Jobs that are perceived as "dead ends," or "unchallenging," usually become former jobs of employees who can neither change nor accept them. Salary can influence a person's perception of a job future, and in times of rapid inflation, a low-paying but rewarding job is more likely to be perceived as lacking a future.

The final area described as a factor in lawyers' decisions to leave their jobs is working conditions. Everything else may be fine, but if you hate your coworkers, or your clients, or your surroundings, you have to go.

The legal profession on the whole sometimes tends to ignore questions involving the personal and professional development of lawyer employees, and, as a result, a concern for the individual's job satisfaction and career development may be neglected. Whatever the reasons for job dissatisfaction, it is undeniable that it is common. It is frustrating to the lawyer who experiences it, particularly if he or she does not know where to turn. This need not be so. The lawyer can always leave a situation that is unattractive and move into something different. For many people, it is not until several years after law school that the best career path for them begins to become apparent. The pre-law student should understand that although a knowledge of legal careers may be useful, it may not be possible to choose an area of practice with certainty.

BUILDING A CAREER PATH

After you leave law school, the work that you do gives you expertise. The tendency in the profession today is to build upon that expertise or specialize. Whether you plan to or not, you will find that the cases you have handled in the past will dictate what you will be able to handle in the future. This functional specialization often parallels formal specialization offered in many states. While requirements vary from state to state, there is a trend toward lawyers practicing in much narrower areas than in the past. It may be that in time, a general practice specialty may evolve similar to the family practice in medicine. The idea that the average person can have someone to call "my lawyer" is not going to die easily.

One of the biggest challenges to the general practitioner is competence. With the law getting more and more complex and clients more and more willing to sue for malpractice, there is great pressure to limit your practice to specific areas of expertise. In addition, the law is always changing, so what you learned in law school ten years earlier may not be enough to keep up with the law.

Continuing Legal Education

Continuing legal education is a multimillion dollar business in which law schools, bar associations, and private groups are all involved. Programs are always being offered to help practitioners stay abreast of their practices. Still, questions are raised about the competence of lawyers at all levels.

The Cutting Edge

It may be somewhat distressing to close on a note of uncertainty, but the fact is that the legal profession is changing and that it is very hard to say what it will be like in ten, twenty, or fifty years, when today's high school students will be getting ready to retire. This chapter has alluded to some of the factors that will shape the profession of the future. If the prospect of entering a field in such a state of flux is unappealing, then consider other occupations. If, however, the prospect of being involved in such a process is attractive to you, law will be an exciting place to be.

As society changes, law and lawyers will be on the cutting edge. Although some critics of the legal profession charge that lawyers spend their professional lives looking backward to precedent and are thus incapable of coping with the future, the obvious reply is that lawyers possess analytic skills that will be crucial if our society is to cope with the future, and that their reliance on precedent is a tool for predicting the future. In a world of change, the career opportunities are vast, and there is probably no career field in our society where there is as much access to these opportunities. Even though traditional jobs for lawyers may be limited, the great flexibility of this degree means that one who is legally trained will probably always be able to find work.

CHAPTER 15

CONCLUSION

DEVELOPING PROFESSIONALS

The professionals—doctors, lawyers, teachers, writers—have always been the intellectual leaders of American society. For more than a few impoverished children, the means to success was through professional education and status. It is, therefore, important that professions be able to attract competent individuals and, when they are trained, to distribute them throughout the population. Ambition must join opportunity for freedom to be fully a reality.

There is a second societal objective in educating professionals, and that is efficiency. Efficiency may sometimes work against the democratic objective, however, because collectively society seeks not only those who want to be professionals, but those who are most qualified. This has been particularly true in the legal profession where the number of persons aspiring to become attorneys has often exceeded the capacity of law schools to educate them. Acceptance to law school is based not so much on desire as on predicted success, which is in turn based on past achievement.

Many students seek a legal education because they see it as an avenue to professional status and financial security. Others come to law with the goal of using their training to make constructive social change. Still others perceive law as an exciting, dynamic profession as legal actions became a routine feature of mass media fare. For these and many other reasons, thousands of students have entered the nation's law schools and later the legal profession. This influx of new lawyers has produced some stress on the system's ability to assimilate them and has resulted in keen competition for jobs. Yet the possible alternatives for developing new lawyers are not that attractive.

The Family Business

One method, historically, of determining occupation has been the use of familial ties. Traditionally, under this system, if your parent was a baker, you became a baker, and so forth. The obvious advantage here was that you did not need to face any disconcerting problem of what to do with your life. Everything was taken care of early, and you assumed direction of the family's traditional work at the appropriate time. The disadvantage, of course, was that if you happened not to concur with the predetermined order of things, there was very little you could do about it. If you wanted to be a candlestick maker, well, too bad; you had to be a baker. Also, society had no assurance that the offspring of any given worker would be the most competent person to carry on the work. A third problem was that if the parents had seven children, there was still only one farm, one business, or one law library. The system therefore established an order, from eldest to youngest, in which the children should be allowed to profit.

Apprenticeship

Another system of training professionals was the use of apprentices. This system was common in the legal profession in the nineteenth century in this country. The master would teach a trade or profession to the pupil, who would supply labor in return for education. After a period, the apprentice could strike out independently. Complex modern society has practically ended the apprentice system in many professions.

Professional Schools Today

It should be noted that family ties still account for a great deal in the business and professional world, and many an individual has followed in a successful parent's footsteps. Apprenticeships, although more apparent in such occupations as skilled crafts, live on. In law, they primarily take the form of internships where a student spends a certain amount of time while in school working in some area related to his or her education. However, professional schools provide a uniformity in the quality of education, probably unattainable under the former system.

The road to a legal career is a long one, and there are many pitfalls along the way. It is nevertheless true that, despite its flaws, the American system of legal education has effectively trained generations of skilled lawyers and will continue to do so. It is also probably true that there are today more opportunities for persons who want to be lawyers than at any other time in this nation's history. Those who want to become lawyers ought not to be deterred simply because the way is difficult. By the same token, those who are not sure they want to become lawyers ought not to embark on this course simply to find themselves.

Hopefully, this book has provided information and insights to those considering law careers, so they can make informed decisions about their futures. A decision as important as the one to become a lawyer, or to pursue any other career path for that matter, cannot be made by reading one book. It must be a choice made over a period of time after reading, talking to other informed individuals, and engaging in much serious contemplation.

You are probably reading this book during a period in your life when you have time to think about law along with many other possible directions to pursue. It is worthwhile in the long run to devote plenty of energy to making good career decisions. This book should have made clear, not only that there are many options within the broad category of law, but also that the path is not for the fainthearted, and finally, that the rewards of a career in law can be substantial.

MODEL RULES OF PROFESSIONAL CONDUCT: PREAMBLE

Adopted by
The American Bar Association
House of Delegates
(1983)

A lawyer is a representative of clients, an officer of the legal system and a public citizen having special responsibility for the quality of justice.

As a representative of clients, a lawyer performs various functions. As advisor, a lawyer provides a client with an informed understanding of the client's legal rights and obligations and explains their practical implications. As advocate, a lawyer zealously asserts the client's position under the rules of the adversary system. As negotiator, a lawyer seeks a result advantageous to the client but consistent with requirements of honest dealing with others. As intermediary between clients, a lawyer seeks to reconcile their divergent interests as an advisor and, to a limited extent, as a spokesperson for each client. A lawyer acts as evaluator by examining a client's legal affairs and reporting about them to the client or to others.

In all professional functions a lawyer should be competent, prompt and diligent. A lawyer should maintain communication with a client concerning the representation. A lawyer should keep in confidence information relating to representation of a client except so far as disclosure is required or permitted by the Rules of Professional Conduct or other law.

A lawyer's conduct should conform to the requirements of the law, both in professional service to clients and in the lawyer's business and personal affairs. A lawyer should use the law's procedures only for legitimate purposes and not to harass or intimidate others. A lawyer should demonstrate respect for the legal system and for those who serve it, including judges, other lawyers and public officials. While it is a lawyer's duty, when necessary, to challenge the rectitude of official action, it is also a lawyer's duty to uphold legal process.

As a public citizen, a lawyer should seek improvement of the law, the administration of justice and the quality of service rendered by the legal profession. As a member of a learned profession, a lawyer should cultivate knowledge of the law beyond its use for clients, employ that knowledge in reform of the law and work to strengthen legal education. A lawyer should be mindful of deficiencies in the administration of justice and of the fact that the poor, and sometimes persons who are not poor, cannot afford adequate legal assistance, and should therefore devote professional time and civic influence in their behalf. A lawyer should aid the legal profession in pursuing these objectives and should help the bar regulate itself in the public interest.

Many of a lawyer's professional responsibilities are prescribed in the Rules of Professional Conduct, as well as substantive and procedural law. However, a lawyer is also guided by personal conscience and the approbation of professional peers. A lawyer should strive to attain the highest level of skill, to improve the law and the legal profession and to exemplify the legal profession's ideals of public service.

A lawyer's responsibilities as a representative of clients, an officer of the legal system, and a public citizen are usually harmonious. Thus, when an opposing party is well represented, a lawyer can be a zealous advocate on behalf of a client and at the same time assume that justice is being done. So also, a lawyer can be sure that preserving client confidences ordinarily serves the public interest because people are more likely to seek legal advice, and thereby heed their legal obligations, when they know their communications will be private.

In the nature of law practice, however, conflicting responsibilities are encountered. Virtually all difficult ethical problems arise from conflict between a lawyer's responsibilities to clients, to the legal system and to the lawyer's own interest in remaining an upright person while earning a satisfactory living. The Rules of Professional Conduct prescribe terms for resolving such conflicts. Within the framework of these Rules many difficult issues of professional discretion can arise. Such issues must be resolved through the exercise of sensitive professional and moral judgment guided by the basic principles underlying the Rules.

The legal profession is largely self-governing. Although other professions also have been granted powers of self-government, the legal profession is unique in this respect because of the close relationship between the profession and the processes of government and law enforcement. This connection is manifested in the fact that ultimate authority over the legal profession is vested largely in the courts.

To the extent that lawyers meet the obligations of their professional calling, the occasion for government regulation is obviated. Self-regulation also helps maintain the legal profession's independence from government domination. An independent legal profession is an important force in preserving government under law, for abuse of legal authority is more readily challenged by a profession whose members are not dependent on government for the right to practice.

The legal profession's relative autonomy carries with it special responsibilities of self-government. The profession has a responsibility to assure that its regulations are conceived in the public interest and not in furtherance of parochial or self-interested concerns of the bar. Every lawyer is responsible for observance of the Rules of Professional Conduct. A lawyer should also aid in securing their observance by other lawyers. Neglect of these responsibilities comprises the independence of the profession and the public interest which it serves.

Lawyers play a vital role in the preservation of society. The fulfillment of this role requires an understanding by lawyers of their relationship to our legal system. The Rules of Professional Conduct, when properly applied, serve to define that relationship.

APPROVAL OF LAW SCHOOLS: AMERICAN BAR ASSOCIATION STANDARDS AND RULES OF PROCEDURE
Selected Standards

STANDARD 210. EQUALITY OF OPPORTUNITY.

(a) A law school shall foster and maintain equality of opportunity in legal education, including employment of faculty and staff, without discrimination or segregation on ground of race, color, religion, national origin, sex, or sexual orientation.

(b) A law school may not use admission policies or take other action to preclude admission of applicants or retention of students on the basis of race, color, religion, national origin, sex, or sexual orientation.

(c) The denial by a law school of admission to a qualified applicant is treated as made upon the ground of race, color, religion, national origin, sex, or sexual orientation if the ground of denial relied upon is one of the following:

(1) a state constitutional provision or statute that purports to forbid the admission of applicants to a school on the ground of race, color, religion, national origin, sex, or sexual orientation; or

(2) an admissions qualification of the school which is intended to prevent the admission of applicants on the ground of race, color, religion, national origin, sex, or sexual orientation though not purporting to do so.

(d) The denial by a law school of employment to a qualified individual is treated as made upon the ground of race, color, religion, national origin, sex, or sexual orientation if the ground of denial relied upon is an employment policy of the school which is intended to prevent the employment of individuals on the ground of race, color, religion, national origin, sex, or sexual orientation though not purporting to do so.

(e) This Standard does not prevent a law school from having a religious affiliation or purpose and adopting and applying policies of admission of students and employment of faculty and staff which directly relate to this affiliation or purpose so long as (i) notice of these policies has been given to applicants, students, faculty, and staff before their affiliation with the law school, and (ii) the religious affiliation, purpose, or policies do not contravene any other Standard, including Standard 405(b) concerning academic freedom. These policies may provide a preference for persons adhering to the religious affiliation or purpose of the law school, but shall not be applied to use admission policies or take other action to preclude admission of applicants or retention of students on the basis of race, color, religion, national origin, sex, or sexual orientation. This Standard permits religious policies as to admission, retention, and employment only to the extent that they are protected by the United

States Constitution. It is administered as if the First Amendment of the United States Constitution governs its application.

(f) Equality of opportunity in legal education includes equal opportunity to obtain employment. A law school should communicate to every employer to whom it furnishes assistance and facilities for interviewing and other placement functions the school's firm expectation that the employer will observe the principle of equal opportunity and will avoid objectionable practices such as

(1) refusing to hire or promote members of groups protected by this policy because of the prejudices of clients or of professional or official associates;

(2) applying standards in the hiring and promoting of these individuals that are higher than those applied otherwise;

(3) maintaining a starting or promotional salary scale as to these individuals that is lower than is applied otherwise; and

(4) disregarding personal capabilities by assigning, in a predetermined or mechanical manner, these individuals to certain kinds of work or departments.

Interpretation 210-1:
Schools may not require applicants, students, or employees to disclose their sexual orientation, although they may provide opportunities for them to do so voluntarily. (August 1994; August 1996)

Interpretation 210-2:
This Standard does not require a law school to adopt policies or take actions that would violate federal law applicable to that school. (August 1994; August 1996)

Interpretation 210-3:
As long as a school complies with the requirements of Standard 210(e), the prohibition concerning sexual orientation does not require a religiously affiliated school to act inconsistently with the essential elements of its religious values and beliefs. For example, it does not require a school to recognize or fund organizations whose purposes or objectives with respect to sexual orientation conflict with the essential elements of the religious values and beliefs held by the school. (August 1994; August 1996)

Interpretation 210-4:
Standard 210(f) applies to all employers, including government agencies, to whom a school furnishes assistance and facilities for interviewing and other placement services. However, this Standard does not require a law school to implement its terms by excluding any employer unless that employer discriminates unlawfully. (August 1994; August 1996)

STANDARD 211. EQUAL OPPORTUNITY EFFORT.

Consistent with sound legal education policy and the Standards, a law school shall demonstrate, or have carried out and maintained, by concrete action, a commitment to providing full opportunities for the study of law and entry into the profession by qualified members of groups, notably racial and ethnic minorities, which have been victims of discrimination in various forms. This commitment typically includes a special concern for determining the potential of these applicants through the admission process, special recruitment efforts, and a program that assists in meeting the unusual financial needs of many of these students, but a law school is not obligated to apply standards for the award of financial assistance different from those applied to other students.

Interpretation 211-1:
This standard does not specify the forms of concrete actions a school must take in order to satisfy its equal employment obligation. The satisfaction of such obligation is based on the totality of its actions. Among the kinds of actions that can demonstrate a school's commitment to providing equal opportunities for the study of law and entry into the profession by qualified members of groups that have been the victims of discrimination are the following:

a. Participating in job fairs and other programs designed to bring minority students to the attention of employers.

b. Establishing procedures to review the experiences of minority graduates to determine whether their employers are affording equal opportunities to members of minority groups for advancement and promotion.

c. Intensifying law school recruitment of minority applicants, particularly at colleges with substantial numbers of minority students.

d. Promoting programs to identify outstanding minority high school students and college undergraduates, and encouraging them to study law.

e. Supporting the activities of the Council on Legal Education Opportunity (CLEO) and other programs that enable more disadvantaged students to attend law school.

f. Creating a more favorable law school environment for minority students by providing academic support services, supporting minority student organizations, promoting contacts with minority lawyers, and hiring minority administrators.

g. Encouraging and participating in the development and expansion of programs to assist minority law graduates to pass the bar.

h. Developing and implementing specific plans designed to increase the number of minority faculty in tenure and tenure-track positions by applying a broader range of criteria than may customarily be applied in the employment and tenure of law teachers, consistent with maintaining standards of quality.

i. Developing programs that assist in meeting the unusual financial needs of many minority students, as provided in Standard 211. (August 1997)

Interpretation 211-2:
Each ABA-approved law school (1) shall prepare a written plan describing its current program and the efforts it intends to undertake relating to compliance with Standard 211, and (2) maintain a current file which will include the specific actions which have been taken by the school to comply with its stated plan. (August 1997)

STANDARD 212. INDIVIDUALS WITH DISABILITIES.

A law school may not discriminate against individuals with disabilities in its program of legal education. A law school shall provide full opportunities for the study of law and entry into the profession by qualified disabled individuals. A law school may not discriminate on the basis of disability in the hiring, promotion, and retention of otherwise qualified faculty and staff.

Interpretation 212-1:
Individual with disability, for the purpose of this Standard, is defined in Section 504 of the Rehabilitation Act of 1973, 29 U.S.C. Section 706, as further defined by the regulations on post-secondary education, 45 C.F.R. Section 84.3 (k) (3) and by the Americans with Disabilities Act, 42 U.S.C. Sections 12101 *et seq.* (February 1993; August 1996)

Interpretation 212-2:

As to those matters covered by Section 504 of the Rehabilitation Act of 1973 and the Americans with Disabilities Act, this Standard is not designed to impose obligations upon law schools beyond those provided by those statutes. (February 1993; August 1996)

Interpretation 212-3:

The essence of proper service to individuals with disabilities is individualization and reasonable accommodation. Each individual shall be individually evaluated to determine if he or she meets the academic standards requisite to admission and participation in the law school program. The use of the term "qualified" in the Standard requires a careful and thorough consideration of each applicant and each student's qualifications in light of reasonable accommodations. Reasonable accommodations are those that do not fundamentally alter the nature of the program, that can be provided without undue financial or administrative burden, and that can be provided without lowering academic and other essential performance standards. (February 1993; August 1996)

STANDARD 213. CAREER SERVICES.

A law school should provide adequate staff, space, and resources, in view of the size and program of the school, to maintain an active career counseling service to assist its students and graduates to make sound career choices and obtain employment.

STANDARD 501. ADMISSIONS.

(a) A law school's admission policies shall be consistent with the objectives of its educational program and the resources available for implementing those objectives.

(b) A law school shall not admit applicants who do not appear capable of satisfactorily completing its educational program and being admitted to the bar.

Interpretation 501-1:
A law school may not permit financial considerations detrimentally to affect its admission and retention policies and their administration. A law school may face a conflict of interest whenever the exercise of sound judgment in the application of admission policies or academic standards and retention policies might reduce enrollment below the level necessary to support the program. (August 1996)

Interpretation 501-2:
A law school's admission policies shall be consistent with Standards 201 and 301. (August 1996)

STANDARD 502. EDUCATIONAL REQUIREMENTS.

(a) A law school shall require for admission to its J.D. degree program a bachelor's degree, or successful completion of three-fourths of the work acceptable for a bachelor's degree, from an institution that is accredited by a regional accrediting agency recognized by the Department of Education.

(b) In an extraordinary case, a law school may admit to its J.D. degree program an applicant who does not possess the educational requirements of subsection (a) if the applicant's experience, ability, and other characteristics clearly show an aptitude for the study of law. The admitting officer shall sign and place in the admittee's file a statement of the considerations that led to the decision to admit the applicant.

Interpretation 502-1:

Before an admitted student registers, or within a reasonable time thereafter, a law school shall have on file the student's official transcript showing receipt of a bachelor's degree, if any, and all academic work undertaken. "Official transcript" means a transcript certified by the issuing school to the admitting school or delivered to the admitting school in a sealed envelope with seal intact. A copy supplied by the Law School Data Assembly Service is not an official transcript, even though it is adequate for preliminary determination of admission. (August 1996)

STANDARD 503. ADMISSION TEST.

A law school shall require all applicants to take an acceptable test for the purpose of assessing the applicants' capability of satisfactorily completing its education program. A law school that is not using the Law School Admission Test sponsored by the Law School Admission Council shall establish that it is using an acceptable test.

STANDARD 504. CHARACTER AND FITNESS.

A law school shall advise each applicant to secure information regarding the character and other qualifications for admission to the bar in the state in which the applicant intends to practice. The law school may, to the extent it deems appropriate, adopt such tests, questionnaires, or required references as the proper admission authorities may find useful and relevant, in determining the character and fitness of the applicants to the law school. If a law school considers an applicant's character qualifications, it shall exercise care that the consideration is not used as a reason to deny admission to a qualified applicant because of political, social, or economic views which might be considered unorthodox.

STANDARD 505. PREVIOUSLY DISQUALIFIED APPLICANT.

A law school may admit or readmit a student who has been previously disqualified for academic reasons upon an affirmative showing that the student possesses the requisite ability and that the prior disqualification does not indicate a lack of capacity to complete the course of study at the admitting school. In the case of admission to a law school other than the disqualifying school, this showing shall be made either by a letter from the disqualifying school, or if two or more years have elapsed since that disqualification, by the nature of interim work, activity, or studies indicating a stronger potential for law study. In each case, the admitting officer shall sign and place in the admittee's file a statement of the considerations that led to the decision to admit or readmit the applicant.

Interpretation 505-1:
The two-year period begins on the date of the decision to disqualify the student for academic reasons. A review, appeal, or request for reconsideration of that decision is in the nature of post-decision remedies. (August 1996)

SAMPLE EXAM QUESTION

This question is typical of an exam question that might be asked on a first-year law school essay exam:

The Central Columbia Power Company (CCPC) provides electric power to some 500,000 residents of Columbia County. Although the public utility has been in operation for over eighty years, the population in the area has more than doubled in the last twenty years. Many new residential communities have been developed in formerly rural areas of the state. In urban Columbia City, most utility wires are deep underground, but in suburban and rural areas electricity is distributed to users through above-ground high tension electrical wires. Although CCPC owns or holds easements over the land on which such power lines are located, in some areas houses and businesses are within one hundred feet of the lines. Predictably, some dwellings predated the lines while others did not.

CCPC has posted warnings at the base of all high tension poles: "AVOID CONTACT WITH THE WIRES" and "DO NOT CLIMB THE POLES." Regular communications to customers by newsletter and media ads advise people to avoid coming into contact with high tension wires and to avoid activities directly underneath high tension lines. Despite these warnings many children find the flat open areas below the wires to be well suited to football, baseball, and other games. In some areas parents even erected playground equipment such as swing sets and sandboxes for toddlers beneath the wires. Other than attempting to dissuade pole climbing, CCPC benignly ignored other recreational activities.

A story in the *Columbia Crusader* (the local newspaper) broke the news that area hospitals were treating an unusually large number of brain tumors in children, many of whom lived and played close to CCPC power lines. The story went on to say that similar statistics occur in many other states, and that research has found conclusively that high tension wires produce electromagnetic fields (emfs), and that emfs are causally linked to cancer. The story suggested that CCPC has known about the emf studies for at least twenty years but has done nothing to either warn customers of the risks or take steps to eliminate the danger.

In actuality, while some scientific studies as far back as 1970 suggested that emfs might be related to cancer, and a number of recent studies concluded that such a link existed, other studies reached a contrary conclusion, so there was no consensus in the scientific community about the effect of emfs. Furthermore, careful inquiry would have revealed that the brain tumor cases, while more numerous than in the past, were not statistically significant.

Among those children who were diagnosed with brain tumors, a parent support group was formed. Representatives from the group met with CCPC officials to express their concern for the children endangered by the high tension lines, to demand that all power lines be insulated and buried to contain emfs, and to seek compensation for those victims who had already succumbed to harm as a result of emfs. The officials denied that any danger was posed by the high tension power lines, explicitly refused to bury or insulate the lines because the cost would triple electrical rates for CCPC customers, and rejected the notion that there was any causal link between emfs and the tumor victims.

Although there is no scientific evidence to suggest that emfs could harm humans through some secondary medium such as food, the extensive publicity given to the "emf crisis" by both the parents' group and the *Crusader,* subsequently reported by other media such as radio and television, produced a generalized fear among the population. As a result, many area businesses near CCPC power lines have suffered loss of revenue. Restaurants, dairy farmers, and poultry producers along the right-of-way have been unable to operate profitably because consumers fear that their products might be contaminated. Several of the restaurants have increased advertising dramatically to bring back their customers, to little avail.

In addition, real estate prices along the CCPC right-of-ways have dropped precipitously, in some cases as much as 75 percent. Some real estate brokers have actively sought out-of-state buyers for these properties since the nonlocals would be less likely to be aware of the emf problem than area residents.

Considering this set of facts in its entirety, what tort actions do you anticipate might be contemplated by individuals and businesses arguably harmed as a result of the events described? Who are the probable defendants of such lawsuits? Who, if anyone, is likely to recover and for what damages? Who, if anyone, is likely to escape liability and why?

GLOSSARY

The following terms used in this book are defined in this glossary for easy reference by the reader. They not only define more clearly expressions used in the text, but also stand to provide an easy guide to "legalese," with which many readers may not be familiar.

ABA—The American Bar Association. A national voluntary association of lawyers with a membership in excess of 300,000 members. The ABA is reputed to be the largest voluntary professional organization in the world.

Accredited Law School—Although the term is sometimes used loosely, an accredited law school has been approved by the American Bar Association through an intensive inspection process; in most jurisdictions only graduates of ABA-approved schools may take the bar examination. Since the ABA is certified by the U.S. Department of Education to grant such approval, only ABA-approved schools can be considered accredited.

Alternative Practice—One of a number of areas of practice that are considered nontraditional. This definition is quite subjective, and the jobs included will vary depending on the individual. Usually alternative practice is a euphemism for legal aid, legal services, and public interest practice (and that is how it is used in this book), although some people also include any law-related employment not in a law firm.

Associate—A junior lawyer in a law firm who is generally salaried, although some associates in some firms may participate in the earnings of the firm.

Baccalaureate Degree—The degree awarded at the completion of a four- to five-year college curriculum; a bachelor's degree (e.g., B.A., B.S., B.B.A., B.F.A., A.B.); the lowest educational level of degree held by students entering law school.

Bar Exam—The test given to law school graduates before they are licensed to practice law; each state has its own bar exam, so law practice is limited to those jurisdictions in which an individual has passed the bar.

Billable Hours—The number of hours a lawyer works and bills to a client.

Career—The sum of an individual's working experience. Generally a career is thought of in terms of jobs, but should properly not be so limited.

Career Development—The idea that a career has a direction or pattern that ideally should reflect the personal and professional growth of the individual as time passes.

Career Options—The choices available to persons in a professional field, generally those positions where one's education and experience prepare her or him for the work that will be involved on the job.

Career Planning—The concept of making rational career decisions on the basis of careful self-evaluation and analysis of the job market.

CLE—Continuing Legal Education. Programs offered to practicing lawyers to update or refine their skills in and knowledge of the law.

Clerkship—1) A position held by a law graduate working for a judge for one to two years after graduation before taking a permanent job. 2) A summer or part-time job with a legal employer during law school doing research and other legal work for attorneys in the organization.

Client—An individual, corporation, government, or other business organization utilizing a lawyer's services.

Clinical Legal Education—Courses in law school in which students handle actual legal problems under the supervision of professors or practicing lawyers instead of merely answering hypothetical or simulated problems; all law schools have some clinical programs but they vary widely in their size, scope, and orientation.

Contracts—A branch of the law involving agreements among people and organizations, including when agreements are enforceable in law and what liability results from their breach; one of the primary first-year law school courses is Contracts.

Corporate Counsel—A lawyer on the legal staff of a corporation.

E-Lawyering—Providing legal or law-related services and information online.

Entrepreneur—An individual who personally establishes and operates a business.

General Counsel—The chief lawyer in a business or government organization.

GPA—The college grade point average is used along with the Law School Admission Test (see LSAT) in selecting students to be admitted to law school.

Group Legal Services—Legal services provided to members of a group (e.g., a union) by staff attorneys as a part of the benefits available to members of the group.

Hanging Out a Shingle—Opening an individual private law practice, either after graduation from law school or after working for a firm.

Hypo—Short for hypothetical situation, a case made up by the law professor to illustrate a point. Example—"Assume that I promise to give you $50 to walk across the Brooklyn Bridge and you agree. Now, when you get three-fourths of the way across the bridge, I change my mind and revoke the offer. Can you sue me for the entire amount? For part of it? For your lost time?"

In-House Counsel—In a corporation or agency, a lawyer or legal department that is on the staff of the corporation or agency, as opposed to outside counsel. A lawyer who works for a private law firm whose client is a corporation.

Internship—A legal job during law school for which academic credit is given, and that usually involves supervision by a professor in addition to the practitioner employing the student.

JAGC—Judge Advocate General Corps. The legal arm of the military services.

J.D. (Juris Doctor)—The basic law degree required to be completed in order to qualify to sit for the bar exam, usually requiring three to four years of study after graduation from college.

Joint Degree—A program in which a law school offers a curriculum leading to degrees in law and another field, most commonly a graduate-level degree in business administration.

Judicial Administration—The management of the court system; a career involving such management.

Law Clinics—Law offices set up to provide inexpensive legal services to people of moderate means by routinizing and standardizing services in such a way as to lower costs while maintaining quality.

Law Firm—A group of two or more lawyers engaged in the private practice of law; the members of the firm are generally called partners, or shareholders, and the salaried lawyers, associates.

Law-Related Job—A job that is frequently filled by a lawyer and for which a legal education is valuable training, but that does not require that the law graduate holding the job be licensed to practice law by passing a bar exam.

Law Review—A journal published by a law school that contains academic analysis of legal questions and recent cases; the law reviews are edited by students who have been selected on the basis of grades and/or writing competition.

Legal Aid—A term frequently used to describe a program offering legal services to indigent or poverty-level clients (see legal services).

Legal Services—1) A general term used to describe the work that lawyers provide for clients (e.g., a lawyer is in the business of offering legal services to clients). 2) A more specific term used to describe a program offering legal services for indigent or poverty level individuals (e.g., the National Legal Services Corporation).

Although used interchangeably with the term legal aid, legal services is becoming increasingly popular despite the confusing definition.

Litigation—An area of law practice involving the trial of lawsuits, the work also refers to any adversary trial in the courts where parties are represented by attorneys in an adversary relationship.

L.L.M. (Master of Laws)—A postgraduate law degree obtained through one to two years of law school after the Juris Doctor (See J.D.).

Local Law School—Euphemism describing a law school's reputation as neither a national nor regional school; a school where graduates are recruited usually by legal employers from the metropolitan area where the school is located.

LSAT—The Law School Admission Test is an exam given to persons interested in attending law school. The LSAT is designed to test aptitude for doing legal work. Although its effectiveness has been disputed, it is used as a major criterion for determining which applicants will be admitted to law school each year.

Median—The middle value in a set of ordered values; thus a median salary or LSAT score means that half the salaries or scores fall above and half below the median.

Model Rules of Professional Conduct—A document promulgated by the American Bar Association nationally, and followed closely in the various states, which defines the lawyer's ethical responsibilities. Violation of these rules may lead to discipline by the authority that licenses attorneys, usually the Supreme Court of the State.

Moot Court—A law school activity involving a competition in which students write briefs and orally argue hypothetical cases before moot court judges.

Multidisciplinary Practice—A firm that includes both legal and nonlegal professionals in the service delivery team.

National Law School—Euphemism describing a law school's reputation as being recognized as one of the best law schools in the nation; a school whose graduates are recruited by legal employers from throughout the country.

Night School—Some law schools have a part-time program in the evening for students who must work their way through school; such a program normally takes four years to complete instead of the three necessary for full-time students.

Nonlegal Job—A job in which a law graduate does not practice law or specifically use his/her law training. Law school may provide a general background and training for the position.

Partner—One of the members of a law firm; the partners are the owners of the business; the shareholders in a professional corporation are sometimes called partners.

Personal Injury—An area of law practice involving litigation produced as a result of some injury to an individual. PI, as it is called, usually involves negligence on the part of one of the parties, resulting in the injury to the other, and in most cases today, insurance is involved.

Population/Attorney Ratio—The population of a given area divided by the number of attorneys in that area; a figure that is frequently used to assess the relative abundance of lawyers.

Pre-Law Major—A student in college who is preparing to attend law school. There are very few schools that offer a course of study in "pre-law" that would lead to a degree as in English or Business, so the term properly describes only the students themselves who may be in any field of study.

Prepaid Legal Services—Legal services provided to persons or families who participate in a plan under which they make monthly contributions and receive benefits designed under the plan. Prepaid legal insurance works very much like Blue Cross/Blue Shield in the health field.

Private Practice—An individual or organization engaged in the business of delivering legal services for compensation.

Pro Bono Publico—(Latin, meaning *for the public good*). A term sometimes used interchangeably with public interest, but also used to refer to the lawyer's responsibility to perform work in the public interest. The organized bar is divided as to the extent and limits of this responsibility.

Property—A branch of the law dealing with ownership of land, objects (chattels), ideas, or anything including what can be owned, and what rights are associated with ownership; one of the primary first-year law school courses is Property.

Public Defender—The attorney who works in an organization engaged in the criminal defense of indigent clients. Since the U.S. Supreme Court case of *Gideon v. Wainwright,* every person who is accused of a crime is guaranteed the right to legal representation. Many jurisdictions fund public defender offices for accused persons who cannot afford to retain private counsel.

Public Interest Practice—A law practice in which the lawyer's clients are not normal paying individuals or corporations, but the public at large; in some cases certain special interest groups promote their causes as public interest (see also *Pro Bono Publico*).

Regional Law School—Euphemism describing a law school's reputation as being recognized as one of the best law schools in a state or region; a school whose graduates are recruited predominantly by legal employers from the region where the school is located.

Skills—In the career choice process, skills are the things that you can do. Think of them as action verbs and as transferable; they represent the things you will be required to do when working in a particular profession such as law.

Socratic Method—A teaching method used in American law schools since the nineteenth century in which the professor, using either written decisions of appellate courts or hypothetical situations, teaches by means of intense questioning of students concerning the cases. Named for the Greek philosopher Socrates, who taught by using a question-answer format, and introduced into legal education at Harvard Law School in the nineteenth century, the Socratic method in recent years has been supplemented in most law schools by traditional lectures, practical or clinical programs, seminars, and problem-solving research courses.

Sole Practitioner—(also solo practitioner). An individual lawyer in private practice.

Specialization—The development of a practice of law limited to a narrow field of expertise, an increasing phenomenon in the legal profession today.

Substantive Law—An area of law practice defined by its subject matter (e.g., energy law, admiralty law).

Taxation—An area of law practice that involves the complex and pervasive federal and state taxation laws.

Tort—(French, meaning *wrong*). An area of law dealing with injuries. Although most tort laws deal with negligent acts that result in injuries, there are also intentional torts and torts in which negligence need not be shown before liability can be established. One of the primary first-year law school courses is Torts.

Underemployed—A term referring to a person who believes that her or his job is not utilizing legal skills adequately. While this term clearly covers those who have accepted nonlegal jobs although they wanted legal ones, it also can be used to refer to anyone who is not satisfied with his or her present job.

Unemployed—In the legal profession, a person who is actively seeking a legal or law-related job but cannot find one and is not employed.

Work Values—Those basic needs and attitudes that determine satisfaction in a professional career choice or job, e.g., independence, power, wealth, altruism.

BIBLIOGRAPHY

This bibliography represents a very short sampling of books about law, lawyers, and legal careers. All the titles were selected because they have something specific to say to the college student embarking upon a legal education.

Most of the books can be obtained through a library or commercial bookstore. Those readers who have been intrigued by the possibility of a career in law undoubtedly will want to read more. In addition to the books mentioned here, several periodicals publish excellent articles about the legal profession on a fairly regular basis. These include: *The American Lawyer, The National Law Journal, The American Bar Association Journal, Student Lawyer, Lawyer's Alert,* and *The New York Times.*

American Bar Association. Section of Legal Education and Admissions of the Bar, *Official Guide to Approved Law Schools*, Chicago: American Bar Association, annual.

American Bar Association. *Standards for Approval of Law Schools.* Chicago: ABA, annual.

Arron, Deborah, L. *Running from the Law: Why Good Lawyers Are Getting Out of Law.* Seattle, WA: Niche Press, 1989.

Bell, Susan J., ed. *Full Disclosure: Do You Really Want to Be a Lawyer?* Princeton, NJ: Peterson's, 1989.

Bolles, Richard N. *The Three Boxes of Life and How to Get Out of Them.* Berkeley, CA: Ten Speed Press, 1987.

Bolles, Richard N. *What Color is Your Parachute?* Berkeley, CA: Ten Speed Press, annual.

Carson, Clara. *The Lawyer Statistical Report: The U.S. Legal Profession in 1995.* Chicago: American Bar Foundation, 1999.

Cooper, Cynthia. *The Insider's Guide to the Top Fifteen Law Schools.* New York: Doubleday, 1990.

Department of Labor, Bureau of Labor Statistics. *Occupational Outlook Handbook.* Washington, DC: United States Government Printing Office, annual.

Lewis, Anthony. *Gideon's Trumpet.* New York: Random House, 1964.

Mayer, Martin. *The Lawyers.* Westport, CT: Greenwood Press, 1987.

Munneke, Gary A. *Barron's Guide to Law Schools,* 14th edition. Hauppauge, NY: Barron's, 2000.

Munneke, Gary A. *Careers in Law,* 2nd edition. Lincolnwood, IL: VGM Career Books, 1997.

Munneke, Gary A. *How to Succeed in Law School,* 3rd edition. Hauppauge, NY: Barron's, 2001.

Munneke, Gary A. *The Legal Career Guide: From Law Student to Lawyer.* Chicago: American Bar Association, 1992.

Munneke, Gary A. *Materials and Cases on Law Practice Management.* St. Paul, MN: West, 1991.

National Association for Law Placement. *Jobs & JDs,* Washington, DC: NALP, annual.

National Association for Law Placement. *1999 Associate Salary Survey.* Washington, DC: NALP, annual.

Shropshire, Kenneth L. *Careers in Sports Law.* Chicago: American Bar Association, 1990.

Stevens, Marc. *Power of Attorney: The Rise and Fall of the Great Law Firms.* New York: McGraw-Hill, 1987.